Beyond Surviving

The Final Stage in Recovery
from Sexual Abuse

by Rachel Grant
Trauma Recovery Coach
M.A. Counseling Psychology

Beyond Surviving
The Final Stage in Recovery from Sexual Abuse

iUniverse books may be ordered through booksellers or by contacting:

iUniverse
1663 Liberty Drive
Bloomington, IN 47403
www.iuniverse.com
1-800-Authors (1-800-288-4677)

ISBN: 978-1-4759-4652-9 (sc)
ISBN: 978-1-4759-4653-6 (ebk)

Library of Congress Control Number: 2012915875

Printed in the United States of America

iUniverse rev. date: 09/06/2012

Dedicated to all of my
Beyond Survivors
past, present, and future

"There is only one thing that will train the human mind, and that is the voluntary use of the mind by the man himself. You may aid him, you may guide him, you may suggest to him, and above all, you may inspire him, but the only thing worth having is that which he gets by his own exertions, and what he gets is in direct proportion to what he puts into it."

—Dr. A. Lawrence Lowell, Harvard

Contents

Welcome

Welcome to Beyond Surviving! I first want to acknowledge you for making the choice to begin this journey of recovery. I personally know how difficult and confronting it can be to look at the areas of your life that, sometimes, you wish you could pretend weren't there. By simply admitting "I need this," you have already taken a huge step toward freedom. Before we get started, I want to share with you a bit of my story and how Beyond Surviving came to be.

I grew up in a fairly small town in Oklahoma, and when I was five years old, my grandfather came to live with my family. I often helped my mom and dad take care of him. I would do simple little things like taking him a bowl of cereal, keeping him company, or reading to him. He was a friend and a quiet companion, up until the day he began abusing me when I was ten years old.

Fortunately, when my parents discovered what was happening, they immediately removed him from our home. Not so fortunately, they weren't quite sure how to support me and help me make sense of what had happened.

My teen years were, as I am sure many of you can relate to, difficult and full of fears about my self-worth and value. I was also confused about relationships and intimacy and felt very alone much of the time, like no one could really understand me.

During my early twenties, I decided enough was enough and began doing all of the things we usually do when we want to get over something—talking to friends, seeing a therapist, reading books. By my late twenties, I was better but was still going around and around the same mountain of self-doubt, anger, acting out, and nonexistent boundaries.

I remember very distinctly the day in 2005 when the thought occurred to me, "I don't want to just survive my life, I want to live it!" That thought stirred something deep inside of me, and I set out to discover how I could live a powerful, authentic life free from the burdens and patterns of thought and behavior that result from abuse.

So, I began reading, talking with others who had been abused, and reflecting on what lessons had really made a difference in my recovery up to that point. I realized that I had come to understand the abuse as an experience, that I had drawn the connections between the abuse and my current behavior—for example, I could explain *why* I didn't trust others. However, there was one critical question that was not being answered by any of the books, therapists, or friends: "So, *what* do I do about it?!"

Beyond Surviving is my answer to that question. It is the culmination of everything I have learned along the way either by experience or through completing my master's in counseling psychology.

I am extremely honored to share my story and to be a part of your journey, and I know there are great things in store for us!

Study Tips

- Don't be too hard on yourself if you reach sections that are particularly challenging, confronting, or that you just outright do not want to do. Be gentle with yourself.

- If you see a video symbol, like the one to the left, this is your cue to go to www.rachelgrantcoaching.com/videos to watch the track indicated.

- A symbol of a piece of paper, as shown to the left, is your cue to refer to a section in the Appendices.

> *If you are reading this guidebook on your own, skip the following and go right to reading "The Philosophy of Beyond Surviving."*

- Make a commitment right now to attend all of the sessions.
- Read the lesson assigned and complete the exercises and reflection questions before the session.
- Review the Homework sections, but do not complete the homework until after the session.

Participating in the Program

(Individual Clients & Course Participants)

Each week we will explore a different area of life that has been affected by the abuse and learn valuable skills for managing the resulting thoughts and behaviors that are particular to each of these areas. You will have opportunities to reflect and practice new skills via exercises and homework assignments.

We will then meet weekly to discuss what you have read and to cover information not included in the guidebook. During these sessions, you will also receive individual coaching meant to address your particular patterns of thought and behavior. If you are participating in a Beyond Surviving Course, I want you to know that everyone in the course will benefit from this time as they listen and apply the lessons and insights of others to their own lives.

Acknowledgments

This guidebook would not be in your hands today if not for the hard work and support of so many people. I know every author says this—but write a book, and you will understand why!

I do want to take a moment to give a special thanks to a few people. It is with love and gratitude that I say:

Rodrigo, thank you for asking the hard questions and pushing me to think deeply.

Sara, thank you for bringing your clear eye, creativity, and gift for making things pop to the design and content.

Idella, thank you for being with me through the whole journey and always keeping the faith.

Cynthia, thank you for your expertise, eagle-eye editing skills, and encouragement.

Laurel, thank you for adding the finishing touches.

J, N, & D, thank you for sleeping through naptime so I could write.

And to everyone else, you know who you are, I am eternally grateful for your support.

The Philosophy of Beyond Surviving

In the world of recovery, there has been a shift from using the word "victim" to "survivor" when describing those who have been abused. This shift shows up in all areas of abuse: domestic violence, rape, sexual abuse, and physical abuse.

This new label was chosen in order to convey strength, to empower, and to embolden us as we begin the journey of recovery. The intent was also to distinguish between the moment of the abuse (victim) and that of the present existence and experience (survivor).

Moving from victim to survivor is an important step in recovery. During this phase, we reflect upon the experience, actively engage in facing and owning what happened, and recognize the connections between the abuse and the way we feel, think, or behave. However, this recognition and sense of empowerment is not enough. While "survivor" is a much better label than "victim," it does not go far enough in framing an identity that leads to a thriving and powerful life.

Imagine with me for a moment that our abuse experience has left a scrape on our knee, like one we might get by falling down on a concrete sidewalk. This scrape, for many of us, remains unhealed for years and years. At times, we may bandage and tend to the wound, but we never fully recover. Worse, we come to believe it never can be healed.

Now, in the case of a scrape, the skin does eventually heal and leave a scar. We look at our knee, see the scar, and remember that day when we were wounded. Yet we do not feel all of the pain or other emotions that occurred at the moment we were hurt. Nor do we continue to compensate for the wound by changing our behavior, such as not fully bending our knee for fear of reopening the wound.

I strongly believe that the wounds of abuse can be healed and looked backed upon in this same way. We can see the scar that was created, but do not feel the pain, need to compensate for, or constantly re-bandage the wound. However, this requires another shift, from survivor to beyond surviving. For that reason, I use the term "beyond survivor" to describe myself, and it is my hope that you will come to describe yourself this way as well.

With this simple shift in language and labeling, the objectives and goals of recovery shift as well. My aim is to support you in reaching a place where you no longer feel it is necessary to manage behaviors or cope with thoughts and feelings that have resulted from abuse. Rather, you will gain insights and skills that make it possible for you to live an abundant, powerful life that is no longer mired in the past. **You will see the scar, but you will no longer feel wounded**.

Let's get started!

PART 1
FOUNDATIONS

Lesson 1
Believing Healing Is Possible

But I've tried to get over this before! Shouldn't I be better already? I know other people have healed, why can't I?

Often the first hurdle to jump over in this journey is to put to rest (or at least put on mute for a while) your inner critic and doubter. I know you've been to therapy, I know you've read books, I know you've tried just about everything under the sun and you are still running in circles. Or maybe you are just now admitting to yourself that the abuse happened and that you need to deal with it. Either way, there is likely a part of you that is wondering if this is really going to work.

I invite you to embrace your inner skeptic—you should, after all, be determining if this is working or not—but by no means give your skeptic the center stage. For a while, allow yourself to embrace this as an adventure, an exploration. **Be curious, check things out**, and try not to stress about end results. We each have to walk our own path of recovery. Sometimes, it takes just one experience to make everything fall into place. Sometimes, it is a variety of experiences.

For me, I tried all sorts of books, therapies, and groups. The ideas that I will share here are those that made all the difference for me. Perhaps this will be the last guidebook you ever do on this topic, or, maybe, it is just another step in the right direction. Regardless, be open to the journey and remember there is a lot to learn from tortoises.

Lessons from a Tortoise

"Adults are always asking kids what they want to be when they grow up, because they are looking for ideas."

— Paula Poundstone

How fabulous is that! I know I am still wondering about what I will be when I grow up, and I know many of the folks around me are thinking about this, too.

For me there are the added questions of "Is it too late?" and "Shouldn't I have accomplished more by now?" I took a bit more time than most to finish my undergraduate studies. Then I spent some time roaming the halls of an elementary school trying my hand at teaching, all while learning a lot about myself.

When I moved to California, I focused on child development (and napping) as a nanny before turning my attention to psychology and coaching. Each stage of my life has in some way built upon the previous one. Most days, I appreciate my wiggly journey. Some days, I agonize about it, because I feel that I am many paces behind those who followed the straight and narrow.

When we feel the pressure to make our mark, crave the pride of achievement, desire to experience ourselves at our best, or want more than anything to be fully recovered, our first point of reference for measuring where we stand is often what others are doing or have done. **Is there real value in this exercise of comparison? It depends on what our ultimate goal is.**

I see at least two possible outcomes from engaging in this sort of reflection. If our goal (though possibly an unconscious one) is to reinforce negative ideas we have about ourselves as being less than, incapable, flawed, etc., comparing ourselves to others is like a gateway drug to self-depreciation. There can be real value in seeing how we measure up to others. But if we cannot compare ourselves to others without becoming depressed, exasperated, defeated, and pitiful, then this is not a healthy choice for us.

However, if our goal is to do something about our current situation and to move forward despite time, age, or circumstances, then it is possible to be inspired, motivated, encouraged, and educated as a result of comparing ourselves with others who have acquired that which we desire. In other words, through curiosity and study of their straight journey, we may add some arrow-like qualities to our own paths.

In my case, I can look to a coach who is my age, has my education, but is much further along, and think to myself, "Damn it, see, if only I hadn't ...," or I can look to see how this person got to where she is and learn—and perhaps learn quickly!

Likewise, we can keep ourselves in a loop of comparing where we are in our journey of recovery relative to others, lamenting that we aren't fully recovered yet, or we can set about doing the work and learning from those who have gone before us.

We only have one life journey. Whether it be a wiggly one or a straight and narrow one, it is ours. So, for all of my wiggly friends out there, move, be active, learn, and don't allow yourself to be distracted by self-deprecating thoughts.

Just as we might discover who we want to be when we grow up from kids, we also do well to remember the lesson of the age-old Aesop fable *The Tortoise and the Hare*. **It's not how quickly you can get to where you want to be, it is whether you get there at all.**

Reflection

How open are you to the possibility of healing?

_____

_____

_____

What gets in the way of you believing you can heal?

_____

_____

_____

How do you compare yourself to others?

_____

_____

_____

Lesson 2
Trauma Is Not a Competition!

"... a man's suffering is similar to the behavior of gas. If a certain quantity of gas is pumped into an empty chamber, it will fill the chamber completely and evenly, no matter how big the chamber. Thus suffering completely fills the human soul and conscious mind, no matter whether the suffering is great or little. Therefore the 'size' of human suffering is absolutely relative."

—Viktor Frankl, *Man's Search for Meaning*

In working with people who have been abused, it is very common to hear minimizing statements such as "It only happened once" or "I know others have suffered worse things."

There is a very real psychological purpose behind minimization—it prevents us from being overwhelmed by the experience and the thoughts and feelings that come along as a result. However, as we reach the place where simply suppressing or managing the effects of the abuse is no longer satisfying, these minimizations need to drop away.

Trauma is not a competition! You don't get fewer points for being abused once as opposed to many times. As Frankl says, suffering, be it great or little, has a way of filling our minds and hearts to capacity ... taking over our thoughts and guiding our behavior.

Rather than trying to escape the impact of the abuse through minimization, we need to take the time to fully acknowledge the extent to which we have been changed or hurt and to what extent that experience is interfering with our relationships and ability to have a life that we love in the present moment.

In doing so, we will be able to deal with the areas of our life that have been impacted rather than remaining stuck, hurt, or angry because we continue to believe that our hurt wasn't "great" enough to justify giving it our attention, to warrant reflection, or, even, to complete this guidebook.

Reflection

In what ways or what areas of life do you feel stuck?

_____

_____

_____

_____

_____

What have you been minimizing and ignoring that you wish you could instead acknowledge and heal?

_____

_____

_____

_____

_____

Lesson 3
What's to Gain?

When we experience abuse, two things are usually occurring. We gain irrational beliefs, pain, anger, distrust ... and we lose a relationship, security, freedom, energy, joy. Recovery is about the journey of bringing back to life all of those things that were lost, deadened, beaten out of you—but not destroyed—as a result of the abuse.

A common thread that ties us to each other as survivors of abuse is the desire to stop certain thoughts or behaviors. We are often focused on what we want to "cut out" rather than what we want to "add in" when we initially start the journey of recovery.

However, I encourage you to spend time reflecting on what it is you would like to "get back" that was lost as a result of the abuse. Knowing what you want to "add in" will get you much further along than focusing on what it is you want to "cut out."

Why is that? **Starting a behavior is much easier than stopping a behavior!** If we think of a behavior or thought as something we have to "stop," we struggle more. I think being told or telling ourselves to "stop" just triggers our inner two-year-olds, and we stubbornly refuse to cooperate.

For example, one client wanted to stop feeling extreme anger every time her boyfriend failed her in some way. As we worked together, we discovered that one of the things she had lost as a result of childhood abuse was the ability to trust that she could depend on others. We shifted away from talking about how to stop being angry and instead focused on what she would need to start thinking or doing in order to trust others. She learned new communication skills. She started looking for times when the boyfriend came through rather than focusing only on the mistakes (which were actually few and far between). She also started to challenge the belief that others would always let her down.

After two months, she was able to respond to being let down or disappointed in a healthy way minus the excessive anger. For example, rather than blowing up when her boyfriend did not come through for her, she would use breathing techniques to calm her body and mind, journal about how she felt in the situation, and then communicate to him the impact his choice had on her and explore options to avoid a similar situation in the future.

As I was thinking about this, I came across this acronym for people who want to stop smoking:

S = Set a quit date.

T = Tell family, friends, and co-workers that you plan to quit.

A = Anticipate and plan for the challenges you will face while quitting.

R = Remove cigarettes and other tobacco products from your home, car, and work.

T = Talk to your doctor about getting help to quit.

START! While the outcome is ending the behavior of smoking, the path to getting there is to start. This same premise applies to our journey of recovery. Focusing on what needs to be added in rather than what needs to be cut out gives us the perspective and the motivation needed to experience real transformation.

Reflection

Can you think of at least one thing you would like to "get back" that the experience of abuse has taken away? What would you like to "bring back to life"? What would be present in your life if you were living instead of surviving?

_____

_____

_____

_____

_____

_____

_____

_____

When the journey gets hard, come back to this list to remind yourself what you are fighting for, what is to gain by doing the work of recovery.

Lesson 4
Integrity and Boundaries

A person of his or her word: someone you can trust because you know they will do what they say they will do

—Cambridge Idioms Dictionary

In the world of recovery, we hear a lot about improving our self-esteem, getting over shame and guilt, forgiving, and a myriad of other areas that are affected by abuse (and, to be sure, we are going to talk a lot about them in this guidebook). Yet the one area I have noticed doesn't get addressed often is the impact of abuse on our ability to live honest, integrous lives.

In the very moment that our trust is violated and we are abused, we have to make a decision. Will we tell or will we cover it up? Most of us, because we are young when the abuse occurs, do not even make this decision in a deeply insightful way. We simply know something about what happened is bad and wrong, and we get in trouble for doing bad and wrong things, so we do not tell.

Then we sit down to breakfast with this huge thing happening that we can't speak about. When asked if anything is wrong, we say, "I need more butter on my pancakes." When someone asks, "How did you get that bruise," we say, "I fell down." Soon, we tell little lies out of habit rather than necessity. This causes a disconnection between what we say and what we are experiencing. We become liars.

Later on, this shows up as an inability to speak up for ourselves, ask for what we need, or honestly communicate what we think or feel about a situation. We feel compelled to conceal, to hide our genuine thoughts, feelings, and, ultimately, ourselves.

As our word, in the sense of a promise, becomes more and more degraded over time, our ability to set and keep boundaries also suffers. We perhaps struggle to say "no," or when we do, find ourselves caving in time and time again. We make commitments that we don't follow through on. We lose all sense that our promises—to ourselves or others—matter at all. The ultimate outcome being that we fail to set and keep boundaries, which leads us to feel guilty, ashamed, or inadequate.

In order to reach a place where we are able to express ourselves authentically and set and keep boundaries, we must restore integrity in our lives. We will start by embracing a very simple definition of integrity—**saying what you mean, and meaning what you say**—then following through with action to see to it that what you have given your word to comes to fruition. For example, don't say "I hate you, I'm never going to talk to you again" if you don't mean it. If you do mean it, then do it! Don't say "We should get together for lunch sometime" unless you mean it. If you do mean it, then send an email or make a call to actually get a date on the calendar.

A word of caution: Our focus on keeping our word (promises) should not become rigid in its practice nor a tool for judging or scolding ourselves or others. Compassion should always underlie our use of any of the techniques or skills shared throughout this guidebook. In other words, when our friend arrives late for dinner, this is not an opportunity to call into question their integrity or character. Likewise, when we break our promises, rather than judging or scolding ourselves, we should get curious about what got in the way of our keeping our word—use it as an opportunity to learn.

As you will discover later, language and what we say is extremely powerful. For too long, we may have been disconnected from our voice. Our language has become a tool for hiding and deception rather than for asking for what we need, setting clear boundaries, or communicating powerfully. So, before we go any further, I want you to consider deeply what you are about to give your word to.

Reflection

Spend some time reflecting on how you are currently using your word. In what areas of life do you notice that you do not say what you mean, mean what you say, or follow through?

_____

_____

_____

If you had to hide or cover up the abuse, what was it like for you to have to keep the abuse secret?

_____

_____

Today, I am giving my word to ...

_____

_____

_____

Homework

Pay attention to how you are using your word this week. Are you saying "yes" but mean "maybe" or "no"? How often is your word aligned with your actions? What excuses do you turn to when you break your promises?

Individual Clients & Course Participants

The Commitments, Guidelines, and Confidentiality forms provide an opportunity for you to take seriously what you are saying "yes" to by participating in the program. It may seem scary, you may hesitate because you are not used to your voice and promises being powerful, but take this step and you are on your way. And don't worry—I am right here with you!

Take some time now to read these over and sign if you are ready to give your word to the principles and expectations listed.

Individual Clients:	**Course Participants:**
See Appendices A & B (there is no Confidentiality form).	*See Appendices C, D, & E.*

PART 2
REWIRING THE BRAIN

Lesson 5
What's That You Say?

"Right speech. We begin now to reach down and take hold of the switches that control our lives. Language is the first. Language does two things: it furnishes both an indication of our character and a lever for shifting it."

—Huston Smith, *The Religions of Man*

This Buddhist concept can also be found in cognitive behavioral theory and rational emotive theory, and it is an amazingly powerful statement that foreshadows the current trend of "positive affirmations." However, beyond the importance of just hearing and saying good things to ourselves, **language has the ability to actually shift our character and experiences**.

When we think about transforming an aspect of our lives, we often focus on what we are *doing* and want to stop. However, the true place to begin transformation is by noticing what we *say* and shifting our language. We need to start new habits around what we say, as opposed to focusing on what we do.

It doesn't take long for us to identify the negative self-talk we engage in daily. Just record yourself talking for ten minutes and you will have plenty of content to work with. Statements such as "I am not very good at most things" or "I am not that pretty" are not just idle statements. They represent the beliefs you have about who you are.

Once you identify these patterns of negative self-talk, how do you then challenge and transform these patterns?

By practicing right speech!

So now, it is time to check in on what you have been declaring about who you are as determined by what you are saying.

Reflection

What have you been saying about yourself? What negative statements do you make about yourself?

Example: I am worthless. I am incompetent. I am never going to succeed.

_____

_____

_____

Homework

Now, on a notecard, on a sheet of paper, or in your notepad app on your phone, write down what it is you would like to know and believe about who you are. For example, "I am valuable. I am capable. I am enjoying life. I am successful." Begin to practice the skill of right speech. **Read this list out loud to yourself every day (carry it with you, glance at it often).**

Pay attention to which words or phrases feel really good and which ones you have a hard time believing or seem unattainable.

Just a reminder here: I am not interested in you just feeling good about yourself or having warm, fuzzy feelings. I am interested in you wielding the power of language to actually shift your character and beliefs about who you are, so that you can live a powerful life free from the negative statements that hold you back.

Saying these declarations out loud is an important first step toward challenging your patterns of negative speech. You may feel awkward or silly, but do it anyway! As time passes, your declarations will become so deeply rooted that it will feel unnatural to believe or say anything else.

When I began this practice, I said daily, "I am valuable." I remember feeling ridiculous and sometimes even laughing out loud at the idea that I could really be valuable. After a while though, by using this practice and others, you will learn in the coming lessons, I finally got it—I am valuable.

One day, a friend of a friend who was visiting and whom I had been getting to know said out of the blue, "You are such a shallow person." I was stunned and surprised, but what happened next stunned me more. I pulled my friend aside and said, "I'm not sure what that was all about, but I'm too valuable to be talked to that way." The words were spoken before I even realized it! I had truly come to believe in my value and, as a result, my behavior and response to the situation flowed naturally from that belief.

Oh, and just in case you don't believe me, check out **"Jessica's Daily Affirmation"** (Track 1) and take a few notes from this little girl—she's in the know!

Bonus: Some of my personal past and present declarations

I declare that:

I am joyful	I am free	I am playful
I am valuable	I am beautiful	I am honest
I am peaceful	I am generous	I am powerful
I am courageous	I am intelligent	I am authentic
I am beyond surviving	I am adventurous	I am vulnerable

Lesson 6
What's On Your Mind?

So far we have learned about the importance of "right speech" and how language has the power to inspire and comfort as well as actually shift our character and beliefs about who we are. Now it is time for the next step in transforming our experience.

Also drawn from Buddhism but found in other theories such as cognitive behavioral theory is the concept of right mindfulness, from *The Religions of Man*:

> *"All we are is the result of what we have thought."*

> Or, as I like to say, *"What you think, you create."*

Now, if we are shaping who we are and as a result what we experience by what we think, then we darn well better be mindful about what thoughts are taking root!

We all have patterns of thought that have been created and reinforced by experiences. The trouble is that these thoughts, while they may have been useful as a way to cope or protect us at one time, become ill-suited for our present-day life. For example, a boy who is abused may develop the belief that he is at the mercy of the demands of others. This belief is quite true in relation to the abuser. However, this belief continues to run in the background even as an adult, and so he is often fearful of being at the mercy of others and pushes back whenever others make requests of him. His thought "I'm at the mercy of others" is causing him to respond to and interact with others in very particular ways and has taken root as a false belief.

Once we identify these sorts of false beliefs (thoughts) that are driving our words and behaviors, how do we then challenge them (in the cognitive behavioral world, they would be called "negative schema")?

By practicing right mindfulness!

What is tricky about how our brain works is that it likes how things are already wired! After enough time, particular thoughts automatically occur in response to certain situations. So, rewiring the brain can be a difficult process when the focus is only on mindfulness.

However, when we bring in the power of language and actually say out loud the new thought that we want to take root, we increase the likelihood of creating new connections and weakening the old ones. Thus, by combining right speech with right mindfulness, we have a powerful combination that can give a one-two punch to the false beliefs and negative statements that are keeping us from living powerful lives.

One of my clients struggled with the reoccurring false belief that she was stupid. The slightest mistake would trigger this false belief and off she went into a whirlpool of harsh thoughts and resulting negative behaviors (e.g., depression, guilt, shutting down). Rather than focusing on the behaviors, we started with her words. Every morning she would say out loud, "I am intelligent and capable." At first, she felt awkward and silly. In fact, her mind was doing what it should do—it was fighting back against this intrusion that threatened to change the status quo wiring. Yet, over time, these words became so deeply rooted, that when she made a mistake, she took it as an indication that she needed to learn more, ask questions, get help, etc. She no longer believed she was stupid. As a result, she began experiencing life, herself, and others in brand-new ways!

Do not allow false beliefs to be in charge. Use the practices of right speech and right mindfulness to challenge false beliefs and break free of old patterns of thought and behavior.

In the previous lesson, I encouraged you to write down what it is you would like to be able to say about who you are and to read this out loud to yourself every day. Now it is time to pay attention to what is on your mind, those unspoken thoughts that are, in fact, running much of the show.

Reflection

What nasty things does that little voice inside your head have to say?
Example: I will never be loved. I am never going to get better. I can't trust people. I am inadequate.

_____

_____

_____

_____

_____

Homework

Spend some time noticing the thoughts that travel through your mind as you go about the day and jot them down. Pay particular attention in moments when you feel challenged, ignored, scared, or insecure. What is that little voice inside saying?

After you have discovered a false belief, write down the positive opposite to create a new thought pattern. Turn "I can't trust others" into "I can be open and trusting." The practices of right speech and right mindfulness will begin challenging and transforming our thoughts to be powerful rather than destructive.

This can be tough work especially when we begin to notice how many false beliefs are running on a loop in the background. Be encouraged, though! Knowing and acknowledging these false beliefs is a step in the right direction.

Lesson 7
It's Nothing but a Neuron!

So, we have been developing the skills of right speech and right mindfulness to challenge false beliefs, but I bet you are wondering, "Where do these false beliefs come from anyway?"

Have you ever walked by a pie shop and, upon smelling a freshly baked pumpkin pie, been transported back in time to a fond memory of Thanksgiving? Or maybe caught a glimpse of a stranger with certain features and found yourself thinking about that girl or guy from way back when? How about a significant other who one day playfully wrestles with you, and all of a sudden you recall being held down by your abuser? What exactly is occurring neurologically and what are the implications for the recovery from abuse?

According to Daniel Siegel in *The Developing Mind: How Relationships and the Brain Interact to Shape Who We Are*, "understanding how trauma affects the developing brain can yield insights into the subsequent impairments of memory processing and the ability to cope with stress." Before exploring this further, let's take a look at how memories are created and recalled in the first place.

There is a saying, neurons that fire together, wire together. When we have an experience, neuronal pathways are created in the brain by neurons firing and connecting to create a neural net. When we smell the pumpkin pie, what is actually happening is that a particular neuronal pathway is ignited. Moreover, this neural net has now been modified. It holds the initial memory of Thanksgiving with family and now the current experience of the same aroma when walking by the store. Thus, **the neuronal pathway is expanded and reinforced by the reactivation.**

Now, consider the implication if, instead of the warm smell of pumpkin pie, the experience is abuse. As Siegel points out, with "chronic occurrence, these states can become more readily activated (retrieved) in the future, such that they become characteristic traits of the individual. In this way, our lives can become shaped by reactivations of implicit memory, which lack a sense that something is being recalled. We simply enter these engrained states and experience them as the reality of our present experience."

This is what Siegel means by "impairments of memory processing." You respond to your significant other in the moment with fear and anger, thinking that what she or he is doing is the problem, when, instead, a neuronal pathway has been triggered and the implicit memory of your abuser restraining you is activated. The same thing occurs in response to stressors. If our experience makes us feel trapped or scared, we may respond in the same way we did when needing to survive the abuse rather than in a way that actually addresses the present-day stressor.

Will we always be held hostage by these firing neurons? Absolutely not! "Each day is literally the opportunity to create a new episode of learning, in which recent experience will become integrated with the past and woven into the anticipated future" (Siegel). **Neurons can be rewired!**

The first step is to simply absorb the fact that many of our present-day responses, thoughts, and emotions are nothing but a neuronal pathway lighting up! Recognition of this creates space for us to consider the possibility that what we *think or feel* is going on may not be what is, in fact, *really happening.*

Secondly, as Siegel states, when one is able to inhibit the engrained state and respond to a situation, trigger, or stressor in a new way, the neuronal pathway will be adapted. The more frequently this occurs, the more modified the neuronal pathway becomes, and the behavior, thought, or emotion that is produced is also modified.

Finally, developing the ability to separate what is actually happening from the interpretations or emotions that follow plays a critical role in our ability to respond to situations in a new way. There are other steps to complete the work of rewiring, but this initial step is critical.

So, let's practice! See if you can identify what happened and the interpretations in this story:

> After a great date, Karen went home and did the happy girl dance. She landed on her couch, excited by the prospect of this new guy, Jim, who seemed to have it going on. He said he would call tomorrow and she was looking forward to it. The next day, Karen stuck close to her phone, but it never rang. By the end of the day, Karen was majorly bummed and essentially decided she was right, no one would ever love her.

What happened:

_____

What is Karen's interpretation:

_____

Now, the very next day, Jim calls her up and apologizes profusely. His phone had been stolen and he had just now managed to get a replacement and track down her number from their mutual friend. I bet Karen wishes she hadn't spent so much time wallowing in her interpretations, which might have been thoughts such as "I'm unlovable, no one will ever want me, people always let me down," etc. Worst of all, she was reinforcing old negative neuronal pathways the whole time!

I have come to affectionately think of these interpretations as "stories," our little efforts at trying to explain or understand why something has happened. Unfortunately, most of the time—like 99 percent of the time—the story we come up with is really just an old neuronal pathway begging to be fed. We usually quickly oblige and find ourselves mired in negative self-talk and self-thought. Our practices of right speech and right mindfulness are tossed out the window.

It is not always easy to separate what happened from our interpretation, but that is okay. Here is your chance to practice!

Homework

In the circle on the left, write down a recent experience or one from the abuse. Remember, you are just writing down the facts of what happened.

In the circle on the right, write down what your interpretation was, what story you told yourself about why things were happening the way they were.

Repeat this exercise three times.

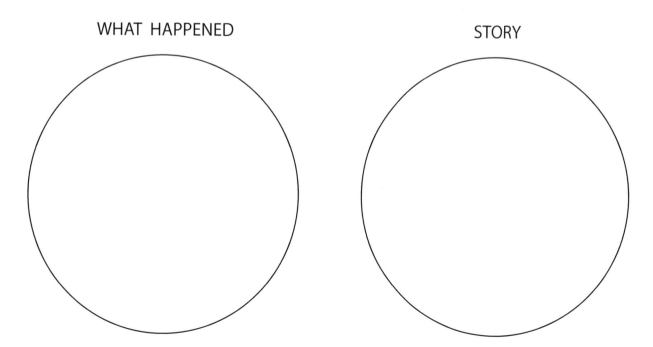

WHAT HAPPENED   STORY

Bonus: One of my stories

The first time my grandfather touched me, I had just helped him out onto the front porch. Usually, he would sit by himself, but, that day, he grasped my arm and held on to me until we had sat down on the swing. I didn't think anything of it in the moment, maybe just that he wanted some company.

I remember being paralyzed for some time, but eventually pulled away and went running to the back of the house to my parents' room. I flung myself across the bed, sobbing, feeling completely scared and confused. I remember thinking "Where is everyone? Why doesn't anyone hear me crying? Why doesn't someone check on me?"

It was in that moment that the false belief "I'm on my own" was created in my effort to answer those questions.

This story has been one that has taken a lot of work to rewire. I started by first getting clear about the facts: What happened was no one heard me crying, no one checked on me. The way that I interpreted the incident, my story, was that I was on my own.

In the next lesson, we will look at the steps for challenging our stories once we have identified them through separating what happened and our interpretation.

Lesson 8
What's the Meaning of This?

"We are all meaning making machines."

I first heard this description of "how we humans work" years ago at a course I was attending. Recently, when I Googled it, I got over 5 million results! Clearly this is an idea that has been floating around and changing the way people interact with each other and frame their experiences for some time. This certainly was the case for me, so let's break it down and figure out exactly what being a "meaning making machine" means.

We are wired to automatically assign a meaning or interpretation to each experience we have. We have a craving to explain why things have gone the way they have. This happens without a conscious effort on our part, but takes root and influences the way we feel and react to any given situation.

Psychologist Albert Ellis developed his theory of Rational Emotive Behavior in 1955. According to his theory, we develop irrational beliefs during childhood that influence our feelings and behavior then and later in life. On a neurological level, the "meanings" are often the same in many situations because an old pathway that was wired long ago is "lit up."

For example, imagine one of your teachers chastised you for a wrong answer in front of the class. Ellis would call this the "actual or activating event." As a way to explain why that happened, you develop the irrational belief, "I'm not smart." Years later, a boss criticizes your ideas and the meaning you assign is—you got it—"I'm not smart." As a result, you may feel inferior, inept, lose confidence, or avoid taking on new projects. The emotional and behavioral consequences are in full swing.

We need interpretations in order to navigate the world and our experiences. However, more often than not, **our first interpretation or meaning has much more to do with our own history, baggage, fears, and false beliefs than with what is actually going on.** As we have learned, the mind likes to reinforce the pathways that are already wired and resists creating new ones. So, when we find ourselves experiencing something that is familiar, the mind will go straight to the interpretation that is already wired rather than make an effort to do something different.

A client of mine recently shared with her husband that she wanted to travel more. The husband responded by saying he needed to do some research before he could make a decision. Immediately, my client took it to mean that he wasn't willing to change or make sacrifices for her, which reinforced one of her other false beliefs, "I am on my own." In that moment, she fell into meaning making, reinforced a false belief, and now, when she returns to the conversation with him about traveling, she will already be set to interpret what he does or says as further evidence that he will not make changes or sacrifices for her.

How do we turn off the meaning making machine instead of greasing the wheels? Well, the bad news is we can't; we are wired this way. However, we can decrease the frequency with which our negative meanings get first priority and decrease how long we stay "stuck" in a meaning once we notice that is what we are up to by using the following steps.

The first step is to identify the bare bone facts of what happened, strip away emotions and interpretations. In the example above, what happened is the husband said, "I need to do more research." Period, end of story. This is a critical first step because it forces us to step away from our meanings and pay close attention to just what was said or done. As Joe Friday would say, "Just the facts, ma'am."

The next step is to determine what story we made up, what was our interpretation. Usually, being quiet for less than a minute will allow the false belief to bubble up to the surface. The meaning in this story was, "He's not willing to change or sacrifice for me." Oftentimes, the meaning we come up with in one situation shows up in many circumstances. So, more globally, my client had a general false belief that "People won't change or sacrifice for me."

Now it is time to challenge the initial interpretation by looking for other possible explanations. Recall Ellis's Rational Emotive Theory I mentioned in the last lesson. He would describe this as "disputing the belief." In this example, my client and I brainstormed other possibilities—"He needs more information before he can make a decision—after all, his personality type is such that he does look for facts and details before making decisions." Or "He's nervous about traveling more since it is not as comfortable for him, so he needs to read more to feel solid about his decision." Or "He was watching football and just wanted to get me out of the way." You see, there are a ton of different interpretations, all of which are possible (and, by the way, her initial interpretation is also a possibility).

What is important to notice at this step is that the initial interpretation is not the end-all, be-all interpretation, which creates room for the false belief to be challenged. By challenging the initial false belief, **we are actually weakening the neuronal connection rather than reinforcing it!** This opens the door to new behavioral and emotional consequences (the final step in Ellis's theory).

With this understanding about how we are interpreting the other person's words or actions, it is time to have a conversation. By going to her husband and sharing her interpretation, she is giving him the opportunity to share more about what is really going on for him so both parties are on the same page. This step is often the hardest, because we are revealing a bit of ourselves. Additionally, it is within the realm of possibility that her husband could say that he doesn't want to change for her. This is one of the main reasons we avoid communicating. We think that hearing the person say something out loud will be much worse than just having the thought running around in our mind. However, if our goal is to lead an authentic, fully expressed life, understanding the needs and wants of the people who we are close to is crucial, even if it stings!

Disclaimer: I am not advising we ignore or completely distrust our interpretations. I am advising that we hit the pause button and check in with ourselves. For example, if someone says they are going to call and they don't, we may initially make it mean something like "I'm not worth their time." In that moment, do the above-mentioned steps to shut down the meaning making machine.

If it is the fifth time that the person has failed to follow through, well now, it is time to notice that our initial interpretation might not be so far off the mark. The only way to find out is to have a conversation. We may find that they have indeed been avoiding us because they are not interested in continuing the relationship or we might find they have lost their job and want to avoid any social interactions. It is very important that, if it is the former, we do not globalize the experience to mean "I'm not worth *anyone's* time." That is a false belief that will cause lots of trouble if allowed to take root.

By the way, determining the root cause or first time a particular false belief occurred may be helpful, but is not necessary when it comes to challenging the story. We can identify and challenge our stories in the present and transform our lives even if we never determine exactly where the false belief came from. The important thing is to identify the nagging false belief regardless of the instigating experience.

So, the next time someone says or does something that elicits a high emotional response, hit the pause button and take a moment to do the steps outlined above and see if there is a false belief that needs to be challenged.

In fact, why wait ... let's try it now!

Reflection

Write about an experience that left you feeling upset, agitated, disappointed, or frustrated. Identify what happened—just the facts!

Example: No one came to check on me when I was crying.

_____

_____

_____

Identify what you made it mean, your interpretation, your story.

Example: I am on my own.

_____

_____

_____

Explore other possible explanations.

Example: My mother was too far away to hear me.

_____

_____

_____

Would communicating with someone about this make sense? If so, what would you say to the person?

Example: "Mom, when I was abused the first time, I ran to your bedroom and cried and cried. I know now that, because no one checked on me, I decided that I must just be on my own. I've been thinking a lot about how that false belief has been impacting me still."

_____

_____

_____

Now that we have practiced challenging the meanings that come up as a result of experiences, let's take a look at what happens when we create meanings based on what people say.

In addition to the experiences of the abuse, we are often told things that are exceptionally powerful or hurtful and shift our meaning making machine into high gear.

Which of these have you heard (or use the blanks to list your own) (from *Shelter from the Storm*)?

- ☐ Why are you making such a big deal of this? You were very young at the time it happened.
- ☐ What did you do to make this happen?
- ☐ You're the problem. You're just using this as an excuse to get your way.
- ☐ Why didn't you stop it from happening?
- ☐ You mean you didn't tell anybody when it happened?
- ☐ Why can't you just forget it?
- ☐ You should just forgive and forget.
- ☐ I don't believe you were ever abused.
- ☐ What is past is past. Let's just not bring it up again.
- ☐ Why can't you hurry up and get over this?
- ☐ I'm so sick of hearing about your needs. What about my needs?
- ☐ You're just feeling sorry for yourself.
- ☐ Can't you just let go of it? Nothing is happening to you now.
- ☐ It couldn't have been as bad as you say.
- ☐ _____
- ☐ _____
- ☐ _____

What meanings or interpretations did you create when these things were said to you?

_____

_____

_____

_____

As Cynthia Kubetin-Littlefield writes in *Shelter from the Storm*:

> *"Sometimes people make these statements because they have absolutely no understanding of abuse issues. Other times the speaker may be mentally exhausted with the survivor or the recovery process. Still other individuals simply may not wish to deal with this difficult situation, because it is threatening to them and consumes too much time."*

Practice challenging one of these meanings or interpretations:

Identify what happened—just the facts!

Example: My boyfriend said, "Why didn't you stop it from happening?"

_____

_____

_____

Identify what you made it mean, your interpretation, your story.

Example: It's my fault.

_____

_____

_____

_____

Explore other possible explanations.

Example: My boyfriend is confused and unsure how to support me.

_____

_____

Would communicating with someone about this make sense? If so, what would you say to the person?

Example: "When you asked 'Why didn't you stop it from happening?' I thought you meant it was my fault that the abuse continued."

_____

_____

Oh, and the bad news is …

In case you are wondering if there is any way to permanently shut down your meaning making machine or stop yourself from "getting into story," let me save you the time and effort you would put into researching that and just say right now, there isn't.

Yes, this even includes me. My five stories listed below are mine—all mine—and they aren't going anywhere.

But, the good news is …

We can **decrease the frequency** with which our stories pop up by weakening the neuronal pathways so that they are not so easily lit up. In addition, we can **decrease the duration** or length of time that we are caught up in meaning making and story by recognizing when we are doing this and using the skills we are learning to pull ourselves out.

Yes, this even includes me. My stories listed below still pop up from time to time, but not nearly as often as they did at one time in my life. I use the steps outlined in this lesson to get out of a story as quickly as possible. Some days, I am quite successful; other days, not so much. Yet each time I do the work of challenging a story, I am weakening the neuronal pathway and increasing the likelihood that I will catch myself sooner the next time.

Homework

Breaking out of meaning making is no easy thing. Moving through the four steps can be tricky, especially when related to some of the core stories that we created as a way to survive the abuse. That's right—our stories actually served us at one point for survival. Yet today, many of those stories are no longer serving us well.

Begin a log of the "meanings" you make this week. You will likely begin to notice reoccurring meanings. Pick two meanings and do the four steps for challenging your meaning making machine.

Bonus: My top five stories

I'm not competent enough to handle this.

People will take advantage of me if I'm vulnerable.

I've got to handle things on my own.

If I'm wrong, I will suffer.

People always leave.

PART 3
ASKING FOR SUPPORT

Lesson 9
Don't Go It Alone

One of my favorite children's books is the *Amazing Mr. Zooty!* In the story, Mr. Zooty comes upon a family that is clearly down and out. Knowing they are good-hearted people, he pretends to faint, and in reward for their quickly jumping to his rescue, he gives each of them a wish. Each wish he fulfills with some added embellishments: syrup for the little boy's pancakes, a hat to match the mother's new purse, and a house to go with the little girl's kitten. When the mother says she doesn't know how she will ever thank him, he simply replies, "Everybody needs a little help sometimes."

Isn't that so true! Yet what we do most of the time is keep our wishes (needs) close to our chests, refusing to share them with others. When we need support, rather than reach out to others, we hide—after all, sometimes it is more important to look like you have it all together than to really have it all together ... right?

No way! One of the things we need to get better at doing is asking for support. **There is no need to go it alone.** This, sometimes, is easier said than done. But why is that?

On one level, we have a general need to look good. We want to be able, competent people who can handle whatever comes our way and so avoid anything that might call that into question. In other words, it is about saving face. This is a natural tendency, but it gets us into a lot of trouble. Things usually tend to get worse rather than better when we retreat and isolate ourselves and do not ask for what we need.

Take the case of one client who lost her job but refused to tell her friends. After three months of going out and spending as if she had a job, she found herself in debt up to her ears. She eventually had to fess up to her friends that she lost her job, hid it from them, and was now in trouble financially—she had compounded things threefold! So much for saving face, right? Now, that is not meant to be harsh, but it is a wake-up call. Not asking for support or trying to hide in the name of looking good is counterproductive.

The other thing that stops us from asking for support is our false beliefs about our own value. Since we have been abused, we question whether we are deserving of help from others. Or, we have the idea that we will be too much of an imposition—after all, how could anyone else handle such "big" problems? Another false idea is that asking for help means we are a failure. These false ideas trap and isolate us from others and need to be challenged and overcome.

Finish this statement: I don't ask others for support because that would mean ...

_____

_____

_____

Whatever is in that blank is the false belief you need to disconfirm or challenge so that you can communicate your need for support to others.

While that may take a little bit of time, we're not going to hold off reaching out. It may feel uncomfortable, you may actually really hate it, but no journey is successful without others by our side along the way. It is important that you have a solid support system around you and that you have a plan in place to contact them should things feel overwhelming as you go on this journey.

So, step one will be to fill out the **My Plan for Managing Crisis Form** (Appendix F) at the back of the guidebook.

Next, do you have a friend, family member, or counselor you could trust enough to share with them that you are participating in the Beyond Surviving program or reading this guidebook and to ask for support? You can tell them as much or as little of your history as you want.

Write their name(s) here:

_____

Reflection

How do you feel about asking for support?

_____

_____

_____

_____

Write about your experience(s) asking for support or help when you were being abused?

_____

_____

_____

_____

Finally, sometimes, we just don't know how to ask for support. The thing is, **we have to be tuned in to or clear about what we really need before we can ask for it from someone else.** Saying to another person "I need some support" is the beginning of the conversation, *not the end*.

What do you mean by support? Do you need someone to just sit with you while you process thoughts or feelings? Do you need help figuring out a solution? Do you need a phone call once a week to check in? Do you need them to call you on a behavior that you want to stop when they see you doing it?

Get as specific as you can about what you need and communicate it clearly. There may be times when you don't know exactly what you need. Be honest and state that this is the case and ask for support in gaining clarity! If we do not ask for what we need or want, we can be pretty sure we will not get it.

Asking for what we really need without vagueness, qualifications, or minimization involves being vulnerable and trusting someone. This can be the toughest part of asking for support. Here's the thing though: Anyone we ask for help has at some point been in our shoes. Don't get fooled by the idea that what we are going through is so different—others have been there, too. It is a bit easier to trust and be vulnerable when we remember we aren't so unique—everybody needs a little help sometimes.

In the next lesson, we will take a closer look at how to make clear requests, a skill we can use when making any request, including this step of asking for support.

Lesson 10
Making Clear Requests

The more I work with clients who want to move beyond the abuse, the more I am aware of one of the greatest hopes we have: that our hurts will not have been in vain, that there is some way to make it matter.

I know we often look to volunteering with organizations, offering our time and energy to support a particular cause, or serving in some other way that contributes to society. This practice is of great value to both the giver and the receiver. Yet what often go unnoticed are the opportunities to serve those who are in our immediate circle, the ones we are closest to, the ones who put up with us during those years of recovery, and the ones who cross our path every day.

Often what inhibits and prevents us from giving or sharing freely with others is a kind of stinginess. This is not the stinginess that makes you give a $1 tip when you know you really should give more. It's not the kind of Ebenezer Scrooge stinginess that causes you to ignore the circumstances of others. Rather, it is a type of stinginess born out of a need to hide and protect ourselves and to preserve a sense of control. Where does this type of stinginess come from in the first place, how does it most often show up, and how can we break free of it?

Human beings are funny creatures. We crave interaction and relationship, yet often behave in ways that directly counter this need. The main thing that gets in the way of us authentically interacting and forming relationships with others is *our need to look good!* How many times have we been in a conversation, and we have no idea what the person is talking about? Yet we nod and agree as if we are also a scholar on Far Eastern spices. When we trip and fall on the sidewalk, our first response isn't "Thank goodness I didn't get hurt," but rather "Did anyone see me fall?" More significantly, we are struggling through a divorce but refuse to tell any of our friends, because we don't want them to think we are a failure.

For survivors, this need to look good is often exacerbated by an experience in our past that made hiding the safest way to keep our abuser(s) away or unable to get at us. Additionally, many of us suffered in silence and worked to keep up appearances to the outside world; looking good was a way to shield ourselves from revealing the truth.

Our egos are important and our need to protect them is also functionally appropriate in many circumstances. However, if we never risk ego by giving up looking good, then we miss key opportunities to share and learn from others, to give others a chance to share genuinely with us, and, perhaps most tragically, to really be seen and known by others. We have to stop hiding.

Another way that stinginess shows up is in our amazing ability to make choices for other people. I am sure we have all experienced the following sort of invitation, "Hey, there's a party this weekend, I'm sure you're too busy to go and wouldn't be interested, but I think it will be a lot of fun—you should come." What in the world is that?!

This sort of non-invitation is used as a defense mechanism to protect our egos from disappointment and rejection. This type of exchange allows us to believe that the person is rejecting the party (because they are busy) rather than rejecting us. The error is in thinking that a "no" to an invitation means the person is saying "no" to you personally. If we can recognize that a person may refuse an invitation for any number of reasons (granted, one of those may be because you aren't their cup of tea), then we can give up the need to protect ourselves by offering these sorts of non-invitations.

Instead, make a clear request: "Would you like to help me on this project?" instead of "I have this project that I would like your help on, but I understand you're probably too busy." Then, accept the person's answer (which, by the way, will often include an explanation such as "Sorry, I already have too many projects") without taking it personally. By making clear requests, you avoid inserting a negative influence that would rob the other person of the opportunity to choose for him- or herself.

Additionally, not asking others for support (e.g., keeping the fact that you are going through a divorce to yourself) is also a type of choosing for others. The people in our lives want to give their support. It is an act of stinginess to deny them the opportunity to love and care for us. So, how do we counter this tendency to choose for others? It may seem simplistic, but when you extend an invitation, filter out anything that is not the clear request. When you need support, ask. Stop choosing for others!

It is a gift to those with whom we are interacting to give up looking good rather than deceptively nodding to avoid acknowledging that we do not understand. It is a gift to let others choose for themselves by making clear requests rather than using non-invitations. It is a gift to others to ask them to support us rather than hiding behind excuses for not doing so (e.g., "I don't want to impose"). **It is a gift to those we love to risk our ego in order to build a more intimate relationship.**

We will discover that our relationships become more genuine and the ones we are with will appreciate our openness. So, stop being stingy! As we search for ways to contribute to the broader society, we must keep in mind those who are close to us. Embrace the opportunities to serve them as well.

We are going to put this into practice by asking for support while completing the Beyond Surviving program or reading the guidebook on your own. In the last lesson, you identified at least one person who you would trust enough to ask for support. Let's work on the clear request that you will make when asking for support.

Reflection

Step 1: Get clear about what you want. What specific type of support do you want or need?
Example: I would like to talk by phone; I want to meet in person.

_____

_____

Step 2: Get even more specific: How often? What day? What time?
Example: I would like to talk by phone once a week on Tuesdays at 12 p.m.

_____

_____

Step 3: Ask for confirmation or agreement.
Example: How does that sound? Would that work for you?

_____

_____

Step 4: Negotiate. Based on the person's response, you may need to adjust the details or you may have to hear them say "No, I can't do that" and not fall into meaning making as a result.

Oh, and the bad news is …

Once we adopt and become skilled at clear requests, we have to give up the notion that others should just "get it." To be sure, we may think that our partner of twenty years should know by now exactly what we want. To some extent, I am sure she or he does. However, last I checked, the power of mind-reading still eludes most of us. So, even if we have a tuned-in partner or friends or co-workers who understand us quite well, there will be times when they will need a clear request from us to know exactly what we need.

Keep in mind, when we see someone with a broken leg, most of us know exactly what needs to be done in almost every single case—scream like hell and call 911. When someone close to us needs attention, support, or comfort—well, things get a little fuzzy. Moreover, being the wiggly creatures we are, what worked yesterday may not work today.

So, give up the belief that others should just "get it" and, instead, be responsible for asking for what you need and being clear about it.

But, the good news is …

By using clear requests, we get in touch with what we really need and take away the guesswork for the person we are interacting with. Additionally, we can objectively determine if the person is following through or not. If we ask someone to "stay in touch," how will we measure that? How will we know if it is happening? If we ask the person to call once a week, that is a concrete, measurable request that can be tracked. This reduces the frustration in communication and allows us to go back to the person to check in on things without it disintegrating into a disagreement about what "stay in touch" really means.

Homework

Make ten clear requests this week. I know this may seem like a lot, but we are constantly coming upon opportunities where we are asking for something. See if you can refine those requests by adding specifics and checking for agreement.

Begin paying attention to how others are communicating their needs or wants with you. If a partner, friend, or co-worker makes a request that is not clear, ask questions to see if you can gain a better understanding of what they need.

PART 4

DEFINING THE ABUSE
& OUTCOMES

Lesson 11
Undoing the Lessons of Abuse

There is a time in all of our lives when we have no concept of what deep pain is. Tragedy is oversleeping on Saturday morning and missing our favorite cartoon. We do not understand the frowns we see on all of the big people's faces. We wonder what could be so bad that they yell, cry, and fight. Life feels light, carefree, innocent, or easy.

There is also a time in all of our lives when we become the thing we could not understand. We find ourselves lying in bed with the covers over our head, afraid to come out and face what is on the outside. We have all had that one thing that caused us to retreat to our beds, to shut out the world, to shut out life. To cry. To yell. For me, that one thing was my grandfather.

I remember the day my grandfather came to live with us. He appeared out of the blue, this short, wrinkled thing that reminded me of the old guy on *Fraggle Rock*. So how bad could he be, right? He always wore this fuzzy brown and orange cardigan. He spent most of his time watching Channel 13, the public announcement station for our small Oklahoma town. All day long, the screen would alter between solid lines of blue, green, and red and bold large print announcing the Bingo Meeting at the Local Union #202, the Pancake Breakfast at St. Mary's Catholic Church, etc. We didn't talk much. I can only imagine the things he had seen and done during his long life, but he took all of those stories to the grave and left a far more interesting one behind.

The moment in my life when my grandfather began abusing me was a beginning, a turning point. To be sure, there were many lessons learned, but the two that shaped me the most were that being vulnerable only leads to trouble and that I had to handle things on my own.

Undoing the lessons learned from this beginning has not always been easy. Yet I tackled them, put them to rest, and "reshaped" who I am. What I came to understand is that we do have a choice in the matter. We do not have to stay broken and burdened.

The fact that we have the freedom to change

> *"... is hard to face up to, so we tend to invent an excuse by saying, 'I can't change now because of my past conditioning.' Sartre called excuses 'bad faith.' No matter what we have been, we can make choices now and become something quite different. We are condemned to be free. To choose is to become committed: This is the responsibility that is the other side of freedom. Sartre's view was that at every moment, by our actions, we are choosing who we are being. Our existence is never fixed or finished. Every one of our actions represents a fresh choice."*

I came across that quote in one of my textbooks. It speaks directly to our journey of rewiring and reshaping who we are. I particularly like the idea that **our existence is never fixed or finished.** In relation to the outcomes of abuse, it can sometimes seem like we are just stuck with these results. Yet, this just is not the case.

As I work with clients, one of the main hurdles to overcome is the idea that we have no choice in how we think, respond, or feel. Whatever our past experiences, we are not condemned to forever be in a fixed state of reliving or rehashing. Sometimes, just noticing that we have a choice in things is a huge first step toward transformation.

One of my clients believed he had no choice about how he reacted to confrontation or disapproval. For example, when his co-worker made an off-the-cuff comment that he had dropped the ball, he responded by railing against this comment for twenty minutes, leaving himself and everyone else wondering why he had been so defensive. He was aware of this and wanted to change this behavior, but was stuck believing it was just how he was built—there was nothing he could do about it.

As we explored his fears and concerns, we found the false belief that was driving his behavior, "If other people are disappointed in me, I will end up alone." This false belief raised the stakes for him every time he experienced disapproval.

He did the work to challenge the false belief so that his reactivity to disapproval decreased. This allowed him to embrace his freedom to choose to respond to confrontation or disappointment in a way that was even-tempered instead of over-reactive.

Reflection

What have you been telling yourself that you have no choice about?

_____

_____

_____

Regardless of where you are in your journey, you have been making choices all along to bring you to this point. Some of those choices may have actually led you to achieving some of the steps in recovery already!

As you review this Indications of Recovery list (adapted from *Shelter from the Storm*), mark items with an * that you believe you are already experiencing, mark items with a ? that you do not understand, and place a ✔ by those that you believe will be particularly difficult for you.

- [ ] I am willing to face the abuse and acknowledge the hurt and the pain.
- [ ] I understand that the abuse was a violation.
- [ ] I have an increased awareness of my value and worth.
- [ ] I can list significant others I can trust.
- [ ] I can share thoughts and feelings about the abuse with others if I choose to do so.
- [ ] I recognize relationship tendencies that avoid honesty and intimacy.
- [ ] I am overcoming feelings of shame and guilt.

I love this snapshot look at some of the things that we need to achieve during our journey of recovery. While it is not a complete list, it is nice to notice that there are probably a few things that you have already achieved in recovery, which means you can heal! Furthermore, you made choices along the way that led you to be able to achieve any of the things you marked with an * above.

Homework

Look at the list you created of things you have been telling yourself you have no choice about. What would you do or say differently if you were to embrace your freedom to choose? Once you have identified what you would do differently, give it a try!

Pay particular attention to the outcomes of choosing powerfully. How does it feel? How do people respond? What becomes possible or present in your life as a result?

Lesson 12
The Abuse and the Abuser

We have just spent some time working on owning and taking responsibility for our choices. So, what we are about to discuss may seem a bit like a step backwards, but it is in fact a crucial component in moving toward Beyond Surviving.

Regardless of when the abuse occurred, there are some critical factors that were at play that prevented us from being able to make choices. Yet we often have a skewed perspective regarding what our options really were at the time for protecting ourselves, blowing the whistle on the abuser, or preventing the abuse from occurring.

The Abuse

Sexual Abuse

Read this definition of sexual abuse (from *Shelter from the Storm*):

> *"Sexual abuse is any sexual activity—verbal, visual, or physical—engaged in without consent, which may be emotionally or physically harmful and which exploits a person in order to meet another person's sexual or emotional needs. The person does not consent if he or she cannot reasonably choose to consent or refuse because of age, circumstances, level of understanding, and dependency or relationship to the offender."*

Reflection

After reading this definition of sexual abuse, what are your thoughts and feelings?

_____

_____

_____

_____

What types of sexual abuse did you experience (adapted from *Shelter from the Storm*)?

I get that checking things off on this list is not the most fun you have had in a while, but take a deep breath and do the work!

Examples of physical sexual abuse:

- ☐ Touching or fondling a child or an adult without consent
- ☐ Excessive tickling and physical restraint
- ☐ French kissing a child
- ☐ Excessive enemas or excessive concern about genital hygiene
- ☐ Intercourse, oral sex, or sodomy with any child or with an adult without consent

Examples of visual sexual abuse:

- ☐ Exposure of a child to pornography
- ☐ Exposure of pornography to an adult without consent
- ☐ Force, manipulation, or coercion of another to observe masturbation or the sexual activity of another
- ☐ Exposure of genitals to non-consenting party or to a child

Examples of verbal sexual abuse:

- ☐ Exposure of a child or non-consenting adult to sexual jokes, teasing, or graphic sexual descriptions
- ☐ Exposure of a child to repeated remarks about the child's developing body
- ☐ Refusing to allow a child privacy for bathing or dressing
- ☐ Name calling of a sexual nature—calling a child a slut or whore is sexual abuse

Examples of covert—without the immediate knowledge of the victim—sexual abuse:

- ☐ Observing another person nude without their consent
- ☐ Videotaping, without their consent, people having sex

Examples of ritualistic sexual abuse:

☐ Forcing a person to participate in religious activities that include sex

☐ Sexual activity that involves chants or incantations

Write about other types of sexual abuse you experienced that are not listed above.

_____

_____

_____

_____

Were you surprised by anything on this list?

_____

_____

Which of your experiences was the hardest for you to acknowledge?

_____

_____

Abusers often try to manipulate the victim by asking for consent or permission. Did your abuser ever ask for your consent?

_____

_____

Which factor(s) prevented you from being able to consent to or refuse the abuse?

☐ Age

☐ Level of understanding

☐ Dependency on or relationship to the abuser

☐ Fear of consequences

☐ Physical strength or intimidation

☐ Other _____

Given the factors that you selected, what are you able to say about your experience that you couldn't before?

_____

_____

_____

_____

Consent is a key component of abuse. When we experience abuse, we often walk away with the idea that we have no choice and that we are obligated to take whatever is dished out to us. It can feel terrible to recognize and embrace that there were many factors at play that prevented us from choosing. The sense of being powerless and at the mercy of another often prevents us from acknowledging this truth. However, while it is true that we had no choice about the abuse, this does not impact our right today to give or withhold consent and to make powerful choices.

Physical Abuse

The National Center on Child Abuse and Neglect defines child physical abuse as: "The physical injury or maltreatment of a child under the age of eighteen by a person who is responsible for the child's welfare under circumstances which indicate that the child's health or welfare is harmed or threatened thereby ..."

Examples of physical abuse:

Biting a child

Hitting a child

Kicking a child

Beating with a belt, shoe, or other object

Breaking a child's arm, leg, or other bones

Not letting a child eat, drink, or use the bathroom

Punching a child

Pulling a child's hair out

Shaking, shoving, or slapping a child

Scalding a child with water that is too hot

Burning a child with matches or cigarettes

Reflection

Describe the types of physical abuse you experienced (if applicable):

_____

_____

_____

Which factor(s) (age, level of understanding, dependency, relationship, fear, other) prevented you from being able to consent to or refuse the abuse?

_____

_____

Emotional Abuse

The National Center on Child Abuse and Neglect defines emotional abuse as:

> "Acts or omissions by the parents or other caregivers that have caused, or could cause, serious behavioral, cognitive, emotional, or mental disorders. In some cases of emotional abuse, the acts of parents or other caregivers alone, without any harm evident in the child's behavior or condition, are sufficient to warrant child protective services (CPS) intervention. For example, the parents/caregivers may use extreme or bizarre forms of punishment, such as confinement of a child in a dark closet. Less severe acts, such as habitual scapegoating, belittling, or rejecting treatment, are often difficult to prove and, therefore, CPS may not be able to intervene without evidence of harm to the child."

The American Medical Association (AMA) describes emotional abuse as: "When a child is regularly threatened, yelled at, humiliated, ignored, blamed or otherwise emotionally mistreated. For example, making fun of a child, calling a child names, and always finding fault are forms of emotional abuse."

Emotional abuse is more than just verbal abuse. It is an attack on a child's emotional and social development, and is a basic threat to healthy human development. Emotional abuse can take many forms: belittling, coldness, corrupting, cruelty, extreme inconsistency, harassment, ignoring, inappropriate control, isolating, rejecting, terrorizing.

Reflection

Describe the types of emotional abuse you experienced:

_____

_____

_____

_____

Which factor(s) (age, level of understanding, dependency, relationship, fear, other) prevented you from being able to consent to or refuse the abuse?

_____

_____

The Abuser(s)

We are going to spend some time now thinking about the abuser(s). Often times, we avoid blatantly naming and identifying who our abuser was and how they abused us. However, by doing so, we are demystifying our experience, bringing it into our reality, and thereby creating the possibility of healing these relationships.

Describe your relationship to the abuser(s) and how she or he abused you. If you didn't know your abuser, what were the circumstances around the abuse?

Example: My mother was emotionally abusive. My uncle was sexually abusive. I was raped by a stranger.

_____

_____

_____

_____

_____

Is the abuser(s) still in your life? If so, how often do you interact with him or her? Reflect on these interactions. How would you describe the relationship?

_____

_____

What kind of relationship would you like to have with this person?

_____

_____

Using the table below, write the name of the abuser(s) and then words that come to mind when you think about that person. Do not edit your thoughts. Write down whatever comes to mind.

Abuser *Example: Uncle*	Words that come to mind when I think of this person are … *Example: Disgusting, pathetic, angry, selfish, destructive*

This may be the first time that you have fully acknowledged and named your abuser and your current relationship or feelings toward him or her. As we move forward in the journey of recovery, we will be exploring how this relationship can be transformed based on your desires and needs.

Homework

Spend some time reflecting on the types of abuse you experienced and those who abused you. Gently become aware of what your experience was like, the things you suffered, and at whose hands. What do you notice, think, or feel?

This can sometimes bring up some hard thoughts or emotions. Be sure that your support person is available before you begin this homework. What other ways can you be safe or soothe yourself?

Lesson 13
Symptoms and Measurable Results

Symptoms

We are going to begin identifying some of the behaviors, attitudes, and outcomes that are very common in people who have been abused. The most important thing to understand is that many of these behaviors served a purpose at one point in time—they helped us to survive the experience of abuse.

As you go through the list below (adapted from *Shelter from the Storm*), check any symptoms that describe your present-day experience and then briefly describe how that symptom shows up for you.

Example: Perfectionism: I spend hours composing emails. I want to make sure everything is perfect before I hit send. I am worried about making mistakes, because I think it will mean I'm a failure.

___ Headaches

_____

_____

___ Sleeplessness

_____

_____

___ Nightmares

_____
_____

___ Sexual Difficulties

_____
_____

___ Low Self-Esteem

_____
_____

___ Lack of Healthy Boundaries

_____
_____

___ Rage

_____
_____

___ Over-reaction to People and Situations

_____
_____

___ Addictions

_____
_____

___ Spacing Out

_____
_____

____ Memory Block

_____

_____

____ Perfectionism

_____

_____

____ Performance/Need for Achievement

_____

_____

____ Repeatedly Feeling Betrayed

_____

_____

____ Fear

_____

_____

____ Withdrawal

_____

_____

____ Anxiety/Sense of Doom

_____

_____

____ Repeated Victimization

_____

_____

____ Anger and Depression

_____

_____

____ Codependency

_____

_____

____ Self-Destructive Behavior

_____

_____

____ Control Issues

_____

_____

____ Others

_____

_____

Bonus: My list back in the day

Lest you become terribly distraught and overwhelmed by the number of things you just checked off, let me share with you my list from back in the day:

> *Sleeplessness, sexual difficulties, low self-esteem, rage, over-reaction to people, addictions (food), repeatedly feeling betrayed, fear, anxiety/sense of doom (always felt uneasy about not knowing how to do things), anger, depression, self-destructive (sabotaged relationships, suicidal), controlling.*

Today, all of these symptoms are either completely gone, or I have the skills for managing when I become "symptomatic." For example, one of the ways I survived and tried to protect myself was by becoming very controlling. I could not control the abuse, so I focused on keeping my room super organized. I thought if I could control my environment then I would be safe. I have learned that this is a false belief (my interpretation or story) and done the work to challenge it.

Still, from time to time, that pile of papers on the kitchen table seems like a nasty dragon that needs to be defeated in order to restore peace and safety to my home. When this happens, I do one of two things: leave it alone and snap out of story or clean it up while reminding myself that I am doing so because I enjoy things being organized not because I am somehow increasing my security. How do I know the difference?

When we are responding as a result of a false belief, **the level of agitation and concern increases exponentially**. By monitoring these levels, we can get a clearer sense of whether our choices are grounded or driven by story.

So, now, let's take a look at how you can begin dealing with your own symptoms one by one until you are no longer being pushed around or dragged down by the effects of the abuse.

Measurable Results

> *"Current research underscores the wisdom of [Benjamin Franklin's] chart-keeping approach. People are more likely to make progress on goals that are broken into concrete, measurable actions, with some kind of structured accountability and positive reinforcement."*
>
> —Gretchen Rubin, *The Happiness Project*

I couldn't agree more, which is why one of the main things we are going to do is create "measurable results," even when it comes to abstract ideas like worthiness, confidence, sleeplessness, depression, or communication. I love seeing things become focused and manageable as we get clear about the small strides we can take toward a larger goal.

So, what exactly is a measurable result? **It is the objective means by which we can measure our progress**. To develop a measurable result, there are a few steps we can follow. The first step is to identify the overall goal. For example: to spend more time with friends. This statement is clear, but it is still way too general to inspire action or be measured. Yet being able to state our goal in a broad stroke is useful as a way to get the ball rolling. We will worry about making the goal more concise later.

The next important step is to identify *why* we want to pursue this goal in the first place. This step often gets skipped or people are unaware of it altogether, but it is actually the most important step in the whole process. It provides the underlying motivation that creates momentum, commitment, and endurance. In addition, reflecting on the "why" is important in order to check in and assure that our reasons are not in some way harmful to the endeavor. So, a healthy motivation might be: to create meaning and deeper connections and to share myself with others. A not so great motivation might be: to prove that people like me.

Once we have identified the goal (what) and the motivation (why), next comes the specific actions we will take (how) and how often (when). Without this step, our goal is likely to remain a nice idea that is never put into action. Initially brainstorm a few ways that you could reach your goal. In this example of wanting to spend more time with friends, you could plan dinners, make a phone call, meet for coffee, or take up an activity together. Settle on one method, action. This is the how. Then decide how much time will be spent each week on this action step. It should be very specific. For example, have friends over for dinner twice a week on Wednesdays and Saturdays.

Next, decide on a method for tracking your progress other than in your head. We are funny creatures in that the times we don't meet our goals stick out to us so much more easily than when we do follow through. So, we need a tangible way to see what is actually going on. You could make a tally chart, mark it in your calendar, have a "friend book" that people sign when they come for dinner. Choose any method that you will enjoy using to track your progress, so that it doesn't feel like more work.

Finally, you need to pick a reward! Oddly enough, this is often the most difficult step for people. For a variety of reasons, we resist acknowledging the good we are doing, the small strides we are taking toward completing a goal. Often-times we buy into the idea that rewards should only come once the entire goal is achieved, but this just isn't so. Positive reinforcement along the road to our goal actually increases the likelihood that we will achieve our aims. So, do not skip over this step. The reward can be anything that you want—buy a new pair of shoes, go for a walk, watch a favorite TV show, eat a favorite dessert. No matter what you choose, give yourself credit for the steps you are taking.

Homework

Choose one symptom and create a measurable result. The example below is a real measurable result created by one of my clients. She successfully reduced her nightmares after only two weeks.

Symptom: _____

Example: I am having nightmares about the rape every night.

Step 1: Identify the overall goal.
Example: To reduce the number of nightmares I have. (Notice we didn't say "Stop nightmares all together." All of us have nightmares from time to time, so be sure your goal is reasonable!)

_____

Step 2: Identify why you want to pursue this goal.
Example: To experience peacefulness and rest.

_____

Step 3: Identify how and how often.

Example: I will have nightmares no more than two times a week, and I will remind myself that I am pursuing this goal in order to gain peacefulness and rest. I will drink a cup of tea to calm myself before bed.

Step 4: Determine how you will track your progress. You could use the **Completion Log** (Appendix G).

Example: I will keep a notebook by my bed and write down first thing in the morning whether I had a nightmare or not.

Step 5: Pick a reward.

Example: I will listen to my favorite music each time I do not have a nightmare.

Now, I want to be clear that the mindset we have after setting a goal and putting it into action is critical. We will not be perfect, and if we allow the times when we do not meet our goal to mean that we will never do it or we will never change, then it does not matter how measurable the goal is, we will lose heart and abandon the goal.

To keep this in check, we can enroll others who will support us and remind us to take one day at a time, practice being forgiving and kind to ourselves, and be flexible. If we are really struggling to meet a goal, then reevaluate, adapt, or break the goal down into smaller parts. Bottom line, **measurable results are meant to help us objectively measure our progress, not our value or capability.**

In addition, a measurable result is not the end-all, be-all of recovery or eradicating a symptom. However, paired with the other skills we are learning—using right speech and right mindfulness to challenge false beliefs, keeping our meaning making machine in low gear—measurable results are extremely powerful, because we let go of thinking that these symptoms or behaviors are just how we are. Instead, we begin to make powerful choices about what we can do differently (either by shifting our focus, adopting new habits, or taking responsibility) to address these areas of our lives that are not working. That is a huge thing!

PART 5

IDENTIFYING & CHALLENGING FALSE BELIEFS

Lesson 14
False Beliefs—The Biggies

As we shift our focus and explore some of the false beliefs or stories that result from abuse, we need to pay particular attention to three of the most common stories that victims of abuse create.

At the time of the abuse, our false beliefs provided protection and helped us survive the abuse, but like in-laws who stay for too long in the guest room, they have outlived their welcome. In order to live Beyond Surviving, we must address and challenge the following false beliefs.

It's My Fault

Of all of the false beliefs, this one seems to take root early on and cause the most damage. We blame ourselves in order to achieve a couple of things. First, if we blame the abuser, then we have to acknowledge that someone we love, someone who is close to us, is capable of doing things that are very bad, cruel, and mean. The image we hold of our parent, caregiver, relative, or neighbor is threatened. It is much easier to stomach being at fault than having to face the reality that those who we trusted could cause us such great harm. Especially if the abuse occurred while we were young, it is extremely hard for the mind of a child to reconcile that the same person who tucks us in at night is also abusing us. In an effort to protect our relationship with the abuser and the world, we blame ourselves.

Secondly, if we blame ourselves, then we can hold onto the idea that there must have been something we did to cause the abuse. Therefore, there must be a way that we can protect ourselves in the future. We believe, "If it's my fault, then I can stop the actions that caused the abuse, and I won't get hurt again." Part of the challenge of giving up the story of "It's my fault" is it **requires we acknowledge that even the people who we are closest to can harm us and that we cannot always control what happens to us.**

One of my clients believed that it was her fault she was raped, because she drank too much and went into the room with the man. She decided that if she no longer drank, she would be safe. This gave her a sense of control and power, and for a while, that was really important to feel. However, eventually the burden and effects of blaming herself took their toll. Once she began to see that not drinking was providing a false sense of security, we were ready to challenge this false belief.

My client first needed to understand that she did not enter a room with a big sign above the door that said "Rape This Way." I suppose had she seen that sign and then walked through the door anyway, then we would need to have a different conversation. This was not the case though! Yes, she is responsible for drinking. She is not responsible for the choice the man made to rape her. Most importantly, **one did not cause the other**.

All of us found ourselves one day being abused. There was no sign warning of our impending abuse. There was no option to choose offered. So, let go of the blame. Place it where it belongs— with the abuser.

Moreover, holding onto this story impacts all areas of our life. Just imagine yourself walking down the street with a big sign over your head that says "It's my fault world!" When someone bumps into you on the street, you immediately apologize (after all, it's your fault). When your husband loses his job, you apologize (after all, it's your fault). When you can't make it to a friend's dinner party, you feel disproportionately guilty (after all, it's your fault). The point I am making here is that you begin to behave as if everything is your fault and life becomes unbalanced.

In addition, the more often you show up as the one who will take the blame for everything, the more the people around you will come to expect this and reinforce your false beliefs by playing the game with you. They will not feel compelled to examine their roles and behaviors because it is expected that you will just let them off the hook by believing it is entirely your fault.

Bringing into balance our ability to acknowledge the part we play while also holding others accountable is extremely important if we are going to live a healthy, powerful life.

Bonus: It used to be my fault

Sometimes, we are able to very clearly pinpoint the moment when a story or false belief was created (wired). For me, I know exactly when I decided that the abuse was my fault.

One day, I was sitting with my grandfather on the front porch (the abuse often occurred there). My mother happened by the window, glanced out, and saw what was happening.

The porch door flew open violently, making a loud crashing noise, and my mother yelled, "Rachel, get in this house!" in her very best "You're in trouble, child" voice. I jumped up from the swing and ran inside the house, convinced I was about to be grounded or spanked. My mother was actually quiet, and I don't remember exactly what came after that.

I do know that, in the moment when she yelled at me to get inside, I decided right then and there that the abuse was my fault.

As I began the work of recovery, I returned to this moment and did the steps to separate what happened from the false belief that was created by first looking for alternative interpretations. Now, it is your turn.

Reflection

False belief (Story): It's my fault because ...
Example: My mother is upset and yelling at me instead of my grandfather.

_____

_____

Truth (What happened):
Example: My mother yelled at me to come inside.

_____

_____

Alternative interpretations:
Example: My mother was scared and just wanted to get me away from him.

_____

_____

For some encouragement in letting go of blaming yourself, watch the clip from **_Good Will Hunting_** (Track 2) and **Staceyann Chin's reading of her poem** (Track 3).

There Is Something Wrong with Me

This particular false belief strikes at the heart of one of the hardest questions we grapple with: Why me? We want so much to understand how it is that we were abused and the person sitting next to us in the coffee shop wasn't. We think, "Surely, there is something engrained about who I am that caused the abuser to pick me."

First of all, given the tragic statistics that one out of four girls and one out six boys have been abused, that person sitting next to you in the coffee shop probably has more in common with you than you think. Keep in mind that these statistics only come from reported cases, so that number is probably much higher!

One of the ways we attempt to make sense of the abuse is by trying to uncover what it is about who we are that caused the abuse. For example, I was an extremely cuddly little girl. To this day, one of my favorite memories of time spent with my father is when I would crawl up onto his lap and play hair dresser. I would "curl" and comb his hair and pretend to give him a shave. Physical closeness came naturally to me; I hugged everyone! When I began trying to understand the abuse, I decided that my being physically affectionate toward my grandfather must have given him the go ahead to abuse me. Some of my clients have believed they were weak, too quiet, or disobedient. Some people even blame their own bodies (genitals) or gender for causing the abuse.

Whatever we come to believe was the cause of the abuse dictates how we then think or behave. I didn't become frigid (as might be expected) as a result of blaming my "cuddliness." But I did withdraw, experienced physical touching only in a very superficial way, and withheld any real cuddling or intimate touching from my partners.

If we blame our bodies, we may eat too much or starve ourselves in order to create a body that won't be desirable. If we blame our gender, we may resist being feminine or masculine. We may come to believe that remaining unattractive will protect us from future abuse or being taken advantage of and so don't take care of our appearance or hygiene. We might become loud and boisterous, unable to enjoy a quiet moment so that no one can make us suffer silently again. We might avoid sex altogether or become promiscuous ... the list goes on and on.

This false belief is extremely heartbreaking to me, **because we lose pieces of who we are in an effort to suppress the parts of ourselves that we hold responsible**. We try to eliminate the attributes that "caused" the abuse in order to control and try to prevent future instances from happening.

It is time to take back who we are by understanding that there is nothing about our character, personality, or appearance that caused the abuse to occur.

Reflection

False belief (Story): The abuse happened to me because I was ...

Example: I was very cuddly.

_____

_____

Truth (What happened):

Example: I hugged my grandfather as any granddaughter would.

_____

_____

Alternative interpretations:

Example: My grandfather's choice to abuse me is in no way tied to who I am as a person.

_____

_____

In case you're curious, I am an amazing cuddler these days!

I Wanted Him or Her to Do This

One of the easiest ways to push away the hurt of abuse and avoid dealing with what happened is to simply decide that we wanted or enjoyed it. Instead of the abuse being something that was being done to us, it is something that we chose. With that mindset, we can maintain a sense of power and control. It is that simple.

The next thing we do is set out to gather evidence that will prove we wanted it to happen. We will decide that we wanted it to happen because we didn't do anything to stop it, we didn't tell anyone, we didn't stay away from the person, and, perhaps most difficult to say out loud, we enjoyed the attention and how if felt at times.

In fact, one of the main things to come up when we explore this particular false belief is the guilt and shame that is often felt because we might have experienced pleasurable physical sensations during the abuse. This is so hard to acknowledge and process, but it is important for you to understand that your body responded in the exact way it is supposed to respond to sexual or physical interactions.

There is nothing that you could have done to suppress arousal. Nothing. However, **your response does not mean that you wanted or were consenting to the abuse.** A bit later on, we will return to this topic to begin the work of separating the sexuality of the abuse from your current choices and responses to sex. For now, let's do the work to challenge this false belief.

Reflection

False belief (Story): I wanted him or her to do this to me because …
Example: I didn't do anything to stay away from him.

_____

_____

Truth (What happened):
Example: Wanting to be close to someone I love does not mean I want to be abused.

_____

_____

Alternative interpretations:
Example: He lived in our house; where was I going to go?

_____

_____

How do you feel after thinking about and challenging these false beliefs?

_____

_____

What becomes available or possible to you once you give up these false beliefs?

_____

_____

The stories you have been telling yourself about the abuse are just stories. It is time to give them up.

Homework

You may notice that there are other false beliefs and stories that have been created as a result of the abuse. For example, I am worthless, people can't be trusted, I am on my own, I can't say no. Spend some time exploring any other false beliefs you identify aside from the three in this lesson. What interpretations or stories do you have to support each of them? Then challenge these false beliefs by practicing looking for what happened and alternative interpretations.

Lesson 15
What Do You Want to Prove?

"One fact of nature is that people have a 'negativity bias': we react to the bad more strongly and persistently than to the comparable good ... One consequence of the negativity bias is that when people's minds are unoccupied, they tend to drift to anxious or angry thoughts. And rumination—dwelling on slights, unpleasant encounters, and sad events—leads to bad feelings. In fact, one reason that women are more susceptible to depression than men may be their greater tendency to ruminate; men are more likely to distract themselves with an activity. Studies show that distraction is a powerful mood-altering device, and contrary to what a lot of people believe, persistently focusing on a bad mood aggravates rather than palliates it."

—Gretchen Rubin, *The Happiness Project*

I couldn't agree more! Much of the work we have done so far has been in an effort to uncover the thoughts we dwell on or persistently return to that cause us to feel angry, anxious, or immobilized. We have been practicing right speech to shift the focus from negative self-talk and using right mindfulness to practice challenging our meaning making machine.

I know, at times, this seems to be an insurmountable task, but one of the ways that we can gain extra footing is to add in the practice of, as Rubin suggests, putting rumination in check. In addition, David Rock and Jeffrey Schwartz point out in their article, "The Neuroscience of Leadership," that:

- **Focus is power**. The act of paying attention creates chemical and physical changes in the brain.
- **Expectation shapes reality**. People's preconceptions have a significant impact on what they perceive.

If what we ruminate upon has a significant impact on how we perceive situations and, moreover, our very brain chemistry, then we need to pay particular attention to what we are focusing on.

Check out the video, ***It's All About Perception*** (Track 4) for a great example of how our focus shapes and limits our perception of reality.

One of my clients who had been sexually abused by her father was out to gather the evidence and prove that all men are rude, uncaring pigs. As an adult woman out in the dating world, she was struggling to find a man who she found pleasing. As we talked about her various experiences with dating, she told me a very interesting story.

On a first date, the man arrived at her door with a small bouquet of flowers. Smiling broadly, he handed the flowers to her (sure he had just earned some major brownie points!). She described feeling angry, closed off, and wanting to just shut the door and cancel the date altogether. She was sure that this man was out to take advantage of her—how dare he bring her flowers as if she was some silly school girl.

As we did the work to understand what was going on here, she came to see that she was so set on proving that men were terrible that she even framed the gesture of flowers on a first date as being manipulative and evidence that he would patronize, take advantage of, and hurt her. Her expectation that all men are out to harm her greatly influenced the way that she perceived the situation.

What we have come to expect of ourselves, others, relationships, and the world is greatly informed by our experiences. The abuse, especially, has shaped our expectations. Ever since the abuse, we have essentially been out to prove that our false beliefs are true. **We gather evidence that reinforces our stories and false beliefs. We ignore all evidence to the contrary.** In other words, we develop tunnel vision.

So now, we have the opportunity to challenge our stories in yet another way—by exploring what it is we have been out to prove and then doing the work to shift our focus.

As my client did the work of challenging her tunnel vision with regard to men, she was able to see that *some* men are manipulative and *some* men are caring and romantic. This is the benefit of challenging our preconceptions—the possibility of seeing the full spectrum of experiences and having a keener ability to perceive what is actually going on.

The critical question is: If anything can be proven true, what is it that you want to prove?

Reflection

What stories or false beliefs have you been proving about yourself?

Example: I am damaged goods.

_____

_____

_____

_____

What would you like to prove instead?

_____

_____

What have you been proving about others? You can write about your significant other, a friend, a parent, a boss … or all of the above.

Example: My husband is lazy.

_____

_____

_____

_____

What would you like to prove instead?

_____

_____

What have you been out to prove about relationships?

Example: People will always take advantage of me.

_____

_____

_____

_____

What would you like to prove instead?

_____

_____

What have you been out to prove about _____?

Fill in with any area of life or relationships where you feel a loss of power—e.g., career, sex, friendships.

_____

_____

What would you like to prove instead?

_____

_____

Homework

Spend this week reminding yourself of what you are out to prove and see how it makes a difference in the way you see yourself, others, and experience the world. Track the evidence that supports what you are out to prove using the **Positive Data Log** (Appendix H).

Lesson 16
Payoffs and Costs

We just spent some time exploring the many false beliefs that arise as a result of abuse and how these shape our expectations, which then compel us to prove particular things about ourselves, others, and relationships. Now, we want to take a look at how we are expressing ourselves based on our limiting beliefs.

There are three distinct ways of being that result from the three false beliefs discussed in Lesson 14:

- As a result of "It's my fault," we experience guilt and self-blame.
- From "There must be something wrong with me," we experience low self-esteem.
- Finally, from "I wanted him or her to do this," we experience shame.

As a result, we fall into

> "... a destructive circular pattern ... between the false beliefs and the resulting emotions. The shameful feelings cause [us] to believe that the shameful beliefs are valid. As this circle repeats itself, it becomes stronger and covers up the real person of value and worth ... [We] ultimately lose touch with [ourselves] in order to survive the pain and loss of abuse."
>
> —Cynthia Kubetin-Littlefield, *Shelter from the Storm*

This results in ways of being.

What do I mean by "ways of being"? **Beyond feelings, it is a way of engaging, showing up, or behaving in the world and in our relationships.** In a variety of situations, we tend to show up as insecure, worthless, incapable, ashamed, or constantly guilty.

While low self-esteem, guilt, and shame are very common ways of being adopted by people who have been abused, there are a myriad of ways of being: the loner, the shameful one, the unlovable one, the pessimist, etc.

What are your ways of being? How are you showing up in the world?

Example: I am damaged; I am undeserving; I am shameful; I am unlovable.

_____

_____

_____

_____

In addition to ways of being, we also adopt certain attitudes or behaviors that impact the way we show up in the world or in the types of experiences that we have. For example, we might have the attitude that "All relationships fail." This attitude impacts how we see ourselves, potential partners, and intimate relationships. Additionally, it may be related to our way of being—the loner—and also show up as a particular behavior (e.g., never attending social events where we might meet someone). It is all one big vicious cycle—one that we are likely hoping to break out of! But how?

The first step is to recognize anything we do is because we perceive there is some payoff. Furthermore, we do not discontinue any behavior until the costs outweigh the payoffs. In the example above, the payoffs might be that we do not have to risk being vulnerable or getting hurt. The costs, however, are that we never get to experience connection and intimacy with another person.

Reflection

What are some false beliefs that have led you to feel guilt, shame, or low self-esteem?

Example: I am unlovable.

_____

_____

_____

_____

What do you think the payoffs are, for you, of reinforcing the beliefs you listed above?

Example: I can remain detached from others and never risk opening up.

_____

_____

_____

_____

What are the costs?

Example: I never get to experience the thrill of sharing myself with others. No one gets to know me.

_____

_____

_____

_____

What are the payoffs and costs of the other ways of being that you identified?

_____

_____

_____

_____

As with false beliefs, we will seek to find evidence to support our way of being. We will adopt the attitude that we are worthless and, no surprise, we will interpret situations to prove this. Worse, we will sometimes latch onto abusive people who help reinforce these false beliefs.

As I mentioned before, we do not change any behavior until the costs outweigh the payoffs. So, the critical question is when wanting to change any way of being or behavior or attitude: Which holds the most weight for you—the payoffs or the costs?

Homework

Use the **Payoffs & Costs Worksheet** (Appendix I) to further identify your ways of being, attitudes, and beliefs. Explore the payoffs and costs of each.

The cost of any behavior can become the motivation (why) for creating a measurable result to begin challenging and transforming a way of being.

Example: The cost of being the loner is never experiencing connection and intimacy.

A measurable result could then be: In order to experience connection and intimacy, I will go out to one event a week and introduce myself to one person. I will track this on my calendar and reward myself by going to a movie.

Bonus: The way to do is to be

One of my favorite quotes comes from the section on Taoism in *The Religions of Man* by Huston Smith (emphasis mine):

> *"With Confucius every effort was turned to building up a complete pattern of ideal responses which might thereafter be consciously imitated. Taoism's approach is the opposite—to get the foundations of the self in tune with Tao and let behavior flow spontaneously. Action follows being; new action, wiser action, stronger action will follow new being, wiser being, stronger being. The Tao Te Ching puts this point without wasting a single word. **'The way to do,'** it says simply, **'is to be.'**"*

Our efforts here to tune in to who we are being is not some idle practice. If we want to transform our experience, bring life into our relationships, lose weight, communicate powerfully, give up an addiction, etc., we must start with our being.

The greatest source and influence of our being is our mind out of which flows our words. Whenever we want to transform a way of being, attitude, or behavior, we must first understand the payoffs and costs and then begin the work of transforming our thoughts and words—our being—out of which will flow "new action" and experiences.

Lesson 17
Shame vs. Guilt

We often experience guilt or shame in regard to the abuse, but are not quite sure exactly what the difference is. So, let's take some time to really distinguish the difference between the two.

Shame

"Shame is the feeling of humiliating disgrace of having been violated. Shame tells you that you are bad."

—Cynthia Kubetin-Littlefield, *Shelter from the Storm*

It can be very difficult to correct feelings of shame, because it becomes a deeply rooted way of being that very much impacts our view of ourselves. For example, "I am unlovable, because I was abused."

Additionally, I see shame as being born out of taking responsibility for something we have "no cause" in. In other words, shame is feeling bad because someone falls down; we feel responsible even though we didn't trip them. Yet we believe on some level that we are bad and therefore must be at fault.

I think of it like a little equation: No Cause + Taking Responsibility = Shame

Reflection

What are some of the words or phrases you use to shame and judge yourself?

Example: I am incapable of doing anything right.

_____

_____

_____

_____

Feeling shame—or taking responsibility for the abuse, something you did not cause to happen—is a defense mechanism. By blaming ourselves, as we have discussed, we are able to deal with the fact that someone we trusted and adored is also capable of harming us in a serious way. However, if we continue to shame and judge ourselves, we are guaranteeing that our lives will be mired in self-abuse, lack of joy, distrust, and lack of freedom.

Based on the judgments you make about yourself, what is the sentence (outcome or future) you are guaranteeing for yourself?

Example: I will continue to sabotage or avoid relationships.

_____

_____

If one of our ways of being is "the shameful one," then we will constantly dismiss our needs or desires out of embarrassment and we will take on the burden of responsibility for things that we had no hand in.

What are you bearing the burden of responsibility for, but are not the cause of?

_____

_____

What needs or desires are you dismissing?

_____

_____

Guilt

"Guilt is the feeling that you did something wrong."

—Cynthia Kubetin-Littlefield, *Shelter from the Storm*

Guilt is related to you being "at cause" for what happened. Guilt is tripping someone and then feeling bad about it. You can correct an action or behavior that leads to guilt. For example, you can apologize for tripping the person.

The equation goes like this: At Cause + Responsibility = Guilt

Guilt is a tricky beast. In its best form, it spurs us on to transform and changes our behavior. In its worst, it can be used as a way to avoid facing reality. One of the payoffs of feeling guilty—of taking responsibility for the abuse—is that we do not have to face the fact that we were powerless.

Reflection

What things do you feel guilty about?
Example: I got into the car even though I felt nervous.

_____

_____

_____

How would you then make amends for these things you feel guilty about (remember, part of guilt is that you can take responsibility and make corrections)?
Example: Make a promise to myself that I will pay attention to my gut and feelings.

_____

_____

If you find yourself struggling to come up with a way to make amends for what you feel guilty about, it is likely that you are trying to take responsibility for something that you are not "at cause" for. Therefore, your guilt is present as a defense mechanism rather than as a call to transform your behavior.

If one of our ways of being is "the guilty one," then we will make ourselves responsible for all that has occurred and fail to see the behaviors and choices of others that have played a role in causing discord, upset, or breakdowns.

More importantly, those around you very quickly learn that this is the role you will play, and so there is little incentive for them to evaluate their own behavior or make any corrections. By being the guilty one, you are essentially letting those around you off the hook and bearing the burden of responsibility on your shoulders alone (this is very much tied to the "It's my fault" false belief). While there may be times when we truly are the only one at fault, if we have a deeply engrained belief that we are at fault all the time, we will not be able to recognize when this is not the case.

What are you not holding others accountable for but instead are taking responsibility for?

_____

_____

As a quick aside, later on we will discuss the process of forgiveness, but unless we move the guilt or blame from ourselves to the abuser(s), we have nothing to forgive him or her for. **They have done nothing wrong if we are to blame.**

Finally, when we look back at what happened, and say things like "I should have known better ...," we are using "retrospective thinking." This means we are taking into account everything we have learned and experienced since that time to judge our capacity to handle the past experience. This is a huge error. How can we expect our younger self to have understood or have had the insights that our thirty-year-old self has? It is very important to remember to evaluate our capacity to handle or respond to a situation based on the knowledge, experience, and life learning we had *at the time* and not from our matured perspective of today.

How are you using retrospective thinking to judge yourself or make yourself guilty?

_____

_____

Now, let me be clear, I am not saying we should never feel guilt or shame! Each emotion has their proper place and exists, in part, to spur us on to better ourselves and to hold others around us accountable. I do want there to be a distinction though between *feeling* guilt or shame when the situation calls for it and *defining* oneself as the guilty one or shameful one. The former brings about transformation; the latter only causes us to stay stuck in patterns of thought and behavior that keep us from living fulfilling, authentic lives.

Homework

Challenge the shame and guilt messages you identified in this lesson by using one of the tools you have learned so far (what do you want to prove, meaning making, what happened vs. story) to transform your thinking and experience.

Lesson 18
Who You Is and Who You Ain't

"Between the ages of twenty and forty we are engaged in the process of discovering who we are, which involves learning the difference between accidental limitations which it is our duty to outgrow and the necessary limitations of our nature beyond which we cannot trespass with impunity."

—W.H. Auden

During my twenties, I definitely did a lot of the work aimed toward answering the question, "Who am I?" I remember it as a time of feeling completely confident one moment and then unsteady and confused the next. There were days when I felt so uncomfortable in my skin. In contrast, these days were balanced by ones in which I easily walked into any situation and felt at ease.

Through a myriad of experiences, I began to discover a person composed of likes, dislikes, attitudes, fears, beliefs, hopes, and weaknesses. I understood myself on new levels and did the work of breaking old patterns of thought and behavior so as to escape the "accidental limitations" that held me back for years. **We have come to understand these "accidental limitations" as our "stories."**

I remember distinctly, a few days after my thirtieth birthday, thinking, "Phew! I'm so glad to be done with that whole 'finding yourself' business." Little did I know! Only weeks later did I realize I had entered a new phase, which I call the "But can you deal with who you are" phase. It became clear to me that the new work to be done was to accept who I was, but also who I was not.

When I came across Auden's statement, it made perfect sense. We have a duty to get past the "accidental limitations" that arise due to abuse, circumstances, or a variety of experiences. Also, it is important to know what is outside of our nature, because not doing so leads to detrimental outcomes. Without this clarity, we chastise ourselves unfairly or waste time on relationships, careers, or other endeavors that we are not suited for.

Reflection

Who are you? What have you learned about who you truly are?

_____

_____

_____

_____

_____

Who are you not? What have you or can you let go of believing about or expecting from yourself?

_____

_____

_____

_____

_____

Even as we give up some of our stories and regain a sense of who we truly are, we may still have a tendency to cover up and hide our authentic selves out of fear of exposure or being vulnerable. Here is a very short and sweet question that strikes at the heart of the matter:

I pretend to be _____ in order to cover up that I am _____.

Over the years, I have heard answers such as "I pretend to have all of the answers to cover up that I am scared to death of being wrong about anything," "I pretend to be generous to cover up that I am really self-centered," or "I pretend to dislike sex to cover up that I want to be touched but am scared."

So, what are you pretending to be?

Reflection

I pretend to be _____ in order to cover up that I am _____.

I pretend to be _____ in order to cover up that I am _____.

I pretend to be _____ in order to cover up that I am _____.

I pretend to be _____ in order to cover up that I am _____.

Pick one of the items from above. If you were to give up pretending, what would then change about the way you are, what you say, or what you do?

_____

_____

In order to live authentically, we need to give up some of this pretending, because, if we continue to cover up and mask ourselves, we are guaranteeing the same outcomes. How can we experience intimacy, if we pretend we don't need it? How can we feel the support of others, if we pretend we can do it all on our own? When we strip away the pretending, we create opportunities for growth and freedom.

For a little more encouragement toward allowing yourself to just be who you truly are, watch **"Be Who You Were Meant to Be"** (Track 5).

We have come quite a long way already in this journey of recovery, and you have taken on some "big-ticket" items when it comes to healing. So, even as you notice that in some ways you are still pretending and not yet living authentically, I want you to take a moment to reward yourself for getting this far.

I will honor the work I have done so far and reward myself by ...

_____

_____

Homework

Practice giving up "pretending" this week, but most importantly, relish the things you have come to know and love about who you are, and reward yourself in some way!

PART 6
EMOTIONS

Lesson 19
Feelings Are Just Feelings

In the following lessons, we are going to do some work around the various emotions that play a big role in the lives of people who have been abused: anger, fear, loneliness, and abandonment. Before we get there, however, I want to set us up to approach these emotions from a very particular place.

First of all, here are a few things to know about feelings (adapted from *Shelter from the Storm*):

- Feelings are neither right nor wrong—only actions can be judged that way.
- Feelings are affected by how we think—negative thoughts produce negative feelings.
- Feelings are often mixed—rarely do we experience one feeling at a time.
- Feelings can be expressed in different ways—there is no one right way; each person has his or her own style.
- Feelings do not lose their intensity by being buried, even for a long time. They must be worked through to lose their punch.
- Feelings should not dictate our lives. Instead, what we have given our word to—integrity—should, at times, guide our decisions.

Let's take a closer look at this list. The first thing to notice is that we should not judge our feelings or experience shame or guilt because we have a particular feeling. Essentially feelings arise for a variety of reasons—from the biological to the circumstantial, some would even argue with the cycle of the moon! So, feelings happen—sometimes terrible, I want to hide-under-a-rock feelings.

Yet if we are to mature into our feelings and manage our behavior, our focus needs to be on the actions that follow feelings rather than trying to eradicate the feeling altogether. For example, if we feel scared in a relationship, that's okay. If we feel scared and then behave miserably toward the other person in the hopes of pushing them away, not so okay! We need to take responsibility for how we act in response to our feelings.

Reflection

What feelings have you been judging as being bad or wrong?

_____

_____

Instead of judging your feelings, what behaviors or responses to your feelings should you instead focus on transforming?

_____

_____

_____

Now, I am sure the second point—feelings are affected by how we think—does not come as much of a surprise to you by now. The more our minds focus on the negative, the more our feelings will follow suit.

In contrast, positive feelings

> "... improve our cognitive capacities while we are in safe situations, allowing us to build resources around us for the long term. That's in marked contrast to the effects of negative emotions like fear, which focus our attention so we can deal with short-term problems. 'Positive feelings change the way our brains work and expand the boundaries of experience, allowing us to take in more information and see the big picture.'"
>
> —Dan Jones, *How to Be Happy*

Essentially, the more positive emotions we experience, the bigger our bank account is that we can draw upon when things get hard. Positive emotions help us see things broadly, while negative emotions create a pinpoint focus. This can, of course, be very useful at times, but not if we fall into a downward spiral of negativity.

How full is your bank account of positive feelings? What could you do to increase your balance?

_____

_____

Finally, we need to remember that feelings are just feelings—they should not dictate our decisions, mostly because feelings are so fleeting! In *Mere Christianity*, C.S. Lewis says,

> *"'the most dangerous thing you can do is to take any one impulse of our own nature and set it up as the thing you ought to follow at all costs.' ... Now no feeling can be relied on to last in its full intensity, or even to last at all."*

If we are slaves to our emotions, keeping our commitments may fall to the wayside over and over again. As a result, our integrity is weakened or falls apart. "I don't feel like it" may seem like a Get out of Jail Free card, but in reality, we suffer and those around us begin to distrust that we will keep our promises. We ultimately damage our relationships and may even be dismissed as unreliable or a flake.

How many relationships end because the initial intense feelings subside and people think, "Hmm, I must not be in love anymore"? How many times do we say no to an opportunity, because we feel afraid? How many times do we bounce from job to job seeking a fresh high?

Too often, we make decisions about whether to stay in a relationship, whether to stay at a job, whether to keep our commitment for a dinner party based solely on our feelings.

Now, lest you label me a hater of feelings, let me be clear that I am not deriding the important role that feelings play in our decision making process. Again, it is about balance—and, for those of us who have been abused—our emotions are often quite unbalanced. We have a tendency to rely too heavily on what we feel. This is particularly dangerous until we move beyond being a survivor, because it is very likely that what we feel is all tied up with false beliefs, stories, and negativity! Until we learn to make balanced decisions, a good rule of thumb is to not let our feelings be the dictator of our actions.

One client discovered that she constantly played the "I don't feel like it" card every time "date night" with her husband rolled around. The day before, or sometimes even the morning of, she would cancel. Eventually the husband became so exasperated, he just stopped offering to take her out. As we began to identify what was driving her feelings, she discovered that she was canceling in order to avoid intimacy. We decided that, regardless of what she felt, she would not cancel the next date night. The evening out with her husband was warm and fulfilling. During our next session, she said, "I wish I had just gone so long ago. It really was so nice to have the time alone with him away from the kids." By keeping her word regardless of her feelings, she was able to experience connection and intimacy and discovered that keeping her word regardless of what she is feeling often leads to huge payoffs.

What opportunities or experiences have you missed out on because your feelings got in the way?

_____

_____

_____

By focusing on what promises we have made, what we have given our word to, we can bolster our ability to follow through or to show up when our feelings would have us do otherwise.

What have you recently been giving your word to but not following through on because of your feelings?

_____

_____

_____

Homework

Honor your feelings—acknowledge them—but practice keeping your word! Pay particular attention to the "I don't feel like it" trap. When your feelings tempt you to break your word, practice noticing the feeling, but following through and keeping your promise anyway. What are the outcomes? What did you discover?

Lesson 20
Anger That Sucks You Dry

Allowing ourselves to experience the feelings related to the abuse, particularly anger, can sometimes prove to be very challenging. We spend much of our time burying them, avoiding them, or looking the other way. We fear that we will just explode, like a volcano, if we express these feelings. Also, we may believe we will not be able to cope or manage if we allow ourselves to really feel these emotions. If we try to approach the feelings, we experience another very powerful feeling: anxiety.

Anxiety acts as a buffer, preventing us from getting to the underlying emotions that we want to avoid feeling, including anger.

Notice though that anxiety is not so much the fear of what will happen or the unknown. It is, however, **the fear that we will not be able to cope** with what might happen. We buy into the false belief that we do not have the capacity to feel these emotions or that we don't know how to handle a given situation. To be fair, perhaps you do have some evidence that you don't have all of the skills in place to manage these tough emotions, but we will work on that! However, in order to decrease anxiety and gain access to these emotions, it is important to challenge the false belief that you are incapable of coping or handling what might come. Let's practice this.

Write about a situation that causes you anxiety or that you believe you can't handle.

Example: Going to a party and not having anything to say.

_____

_____

_____

_____

Now, imagine what you would do if what causes you anxiety actually occurs.

Example: I would ask people questions about themselves rather than trying to come up with something to say.

_____

_____

Next, imagine the worst possible outcome.

Example: I don't talk to anyone all night.

_____

_____

What would you do if that happened?

Example: I would enjoy the party as much as possible without making it mean that I am a loser.

_____

_____

As we project into the future and explore all of the different things that might happen and how we would handle it, our anxiety actually decreases. We realize we have the capability of handling almost any situation that might come across our doorstep. We either already know what to do or we know how to ask for support.

By removing this "anxiety buffer," we are better able to approach and experience our emotions, particularly anger. As we explore the anger we feel around the abuse, remember not to judge the feeling. We are quite justified in feeling angry. However, the work to be done here is to explore how we behave as a result of our anger, where our anger is getting in the way of us keeping our word, and what we can do to balance the anger with positive emotions.

Reflection

Use the exercise above to explore your ability to cope with anger. What do you believe might happen if you express your anger? What would you do?

_____

_____

_____

_____

Feeling anger toward the abuser and acknowledging that anger is absolutely allowed. This particular emotion is often expressed in a variety of healthy and unhealthy ways. As you explore your anger, pay particular attention to the ways you can eliminate unhealthy responses and cultivate healthy ways of coping.

What are some of the unhealthy ways that you respond to anger? Which behaviors do you need to put in check?

Example: Throw things, yell, stuff it, perfectionism, make nice, turn it on myself.

_____

_____

What ways have you seen others express anger?

_____

_____

How do you bury, avoid, or stuff your feelings?

_____

_____

What other emotions (e.g., hurt, rejection, shame, humiliation, loneliness, etc.) do you think your anger is covering up?

_____

_____

Do you tend to turn anger inward and blame yourself or turn anger outward and blame others?

_____

_____

Is there any one thing about the abuse that makes you feel particularly angry?

_____

_____

What are the healthy ways that you already know for coping with anger?

_____

_____

How can you further cultivate healthy coping strategies to use when you feel angry?

_____

_____

How is anger preventing you from keeping your word?

_____

_____

How can anger be beneficial?

_____

_____

If you were to give yourself permission to feel angry, what would you say to yourself?

_____

_____

Homework

Now that you have given yourself permission to feel and express your anger, write a "spew" letter. Maybe you have never allowed yourself to say out loud (or on paper in this case) all of the things that really piss you off. Here is your chance! Allow yourself to rant about all of the things you are angry about with regard to the abuse.

Before you begin, however, it is important that you give some thought to how you will keep yourself safe during this exercise. How will you pamper and soothe yourself afterwards?

Bonus: I was one angry redhead

Of all of the emotions that I have experienced as a result of the abuse, anger—well, really, rage—has been the thorn in my side.

After my mother discovered what was going on, she and my father were great. They immediately removed my grandfather from the house and got me into counseling. Around week three of counseling, the therapist asked me what it was I thought had caused the abuse. Here I am, a little ten-year-old girl being asked to explain what I still cannot explain to this day!* I was so angry I stormed out of the office and refused to go back. My parents were dismayed and tried to get me to see other therapists, but I was not having it. Not really sure how to handle things, my parents, in my view, simply withdrew from the battle.

This left me feeling abandoned and further reinforced my story that I had to make my way on my own. From that point on, I was on the defensive, ready to attack. I would have outbursts of anger that included slamming doors, breaking things, and even sometimes hurting my own body. It was not a pretty picture.

The raging continued well into my twenties. One day, I sat down and wrote my own "spew" letter. I let fall onto paper all of the fears I had about being alone, being rejected, the hatred I felt for my abuser, and the lack of connection I had felt in my life.

Eight pages and lots of tears later, I was met with one very profound realization: My life was being sucked dry by the anger. That day, I decided enough was enough and made a commitment to have peacefulness and joy in my life. My first step was to start saying out loud every day, "I am peaceful and joyful." When I started, the words felt like steel wool on my tongue. After a month, I could say it and partially believe it. After three months, I felt a sense of ease and comfort that I had thought I would never feel again. After six months, I was no longer filled with rage. Of course, it wasn't all just about the words. I had to challenge my stories about being abandoned, rejected, and alone, too.

Today, I still "go redhead" from time to time, but I never rage in the way I used to when I felt the world was out to get me and I had to fight with everything inside of me to survive. These days, I go for a walk, read a book, or take a nap until I feel grounded and able to process what is going on. And, yes, sometimes, I manage perfectly. Other days, not so much. Either way, I know that my feelings are just feelings, and I can choose how I will respond.

Notice how that moment in the therapist's office is so filled with story. He asked me a question, and, while perhaps not put very well, I immediately latched on to the idea that he, too, thought it was my fault and just wanted me to admit it. Even back then, my stories were in play.

Lesson 21
Fear That Keeps You Stuck

"Loneliness and fear are common feelings for survivors of sexual abuse. For survivors to begin to shut themselves away emotionally and sometimes physically is normal because they have been hurt, and the world no longer feels like a safe place. When something hurts you, to be afraid of that source of pain is normal. However, the fear and isolation begin to create more fear and loneliness—feelings that are unrelated to the original abuse."

—Cynthia Kubetin-Littlefield, *Shelter from the Storm*

Really read that last line, "feelings that are unrelated to the original abuse." One of the hardest things about being afraid is that fear takes on a life of its own. A single moment—one dog nipping at you—becomes a fear of all dogs. One person hurting you becomes a fear that everyone will hurt you. Our fears are not to be taken lightly. They can be so strong that they immobilize us.

We will get to loneliness in the next lesson. For now, let's take a look at the fears that are keeping you stuck.

Reflection

List your fears:
Example: being attacked, never being loved, never succeed at healing, sharing myself with others, crowds, being alone.

_____

_____

_____

How do you run away from your fears?

_____

_____

How do you face your fears?

_____

_____

As a result of these fears, what are you missing out on, unable to do?

_____

_____

What are the payoffs and costs of your fears?

_____

_____

"Many a false step was made by standing still."

—Fortune cookie

When we are struggling to break out of our fears, it often seems safer and easier to just stick with the status quo. There is something comforting about the familiar. Yet we will find ourselves in a moment when we can take a step forward or simply keep our feet planted. The choice we make at such defining moments is crucial.

Reasons for standing still are numerous. Movement creates momentum and we can be unsure or afraid of where that momentum might take us. We may feel a bit unsteady when we take some new, first steps—kinda like toddlers fumbling around. Those "fumbly" steps are so critical though. Without them, we never have the opportunity to experience leaping, running, or dancing!

There is very little to gain from standing still.

Now I am not talking about the kind of stillness that comes from being peaceful or making decisions with foresight and thoughtfulness.

What I do want to challenge is the idea that standing still is the "safe" choice. How can allowing our feet to become rooted in the ground be safe? It seems to me, if we are firmly planted, we are much more vulnerable to those who can approach and use us as they will.

It is time to uproot ourselves! To shed the distorted thinking, memories, and fears that immobilize us.

I once had a client who was afraid of sharing herself with others. She believed doing so would open her up to being taken advantage of. When she was with a group of women, she sat quietly almost the entire time, except for asking questions occasionally. This had become such the norm for her that thinking about doing something different caused her fear and anxiety. Yet she was craving deeper female friendships.

After exploring the payoffs and costs of this fear, she decided it was time to step out into new possibilities and try on expressing herself. The next week, at her daughter's soccer game, she approached one of the moms and asked her out for coffee. The woman replied, "Oh, I'm so glad you asked! I've been meaning to ask you out for some time."

Not only does this experience illustrate the personal rewards of challenging our fears, but it also highlights something very important. When we challenge our own fears, we also create opportunities for others to break free as well. I can just imagine the other mom in her own struggle to reach out maybe because of her fear of being rejected. Remember everyone has fears.

Homework

Pick one of the fears you listed. Identify the payoffs and costs of that particular fear. Next, create a measurable result that will move you into action to challenge the fear. What would your first step be?

Example: I am afraid I will be attacked.

Payoff: I can isolate myself from others and not have to connect with anyone, because I stay isolated and very seldom go out.

Costs: I am so worried when I do go out that I can never relax and enjoy my friends.

Measurable Result: In order to feel relaxed and enjoy my friends, I will go out once a week. I will write about what happens when I am out (gather evidence to counter my false belief). I will track my nights out in my journal and reward myself with a warm cup of tea when I get home.

Lesson 22
Loneliness

When I was twelve years old, I went to one of the many slumber parties that sprinkled my childhood days. I was super excited to be going to this particular slumber party because my best friend was the hostess. She lived next door (so there was the added comfort that I could just go home if things went wrong). We had spent lots of time together playing in the wide open fields behind our houses, so I was at ease about going to the party knowing that there was at least one person there I could have fun with.

This definitely was not always the case. After the abuse, I remember days when it felt like all of the color had been drained out of the world. I would watch my peers play with their dolls and even beginning to gossip about which boy they thought was the cutest in the class. In those moments, I felt like a complete outsider. I wanted to scream at them, "How can you be so silly? Don't you know really bad things happen in this world?!" I felt alone and like I just did not belong with these girls. This feeling has stayed with me through the years, even as the conversation has gone from cute boys to, well, cute men.

Abuse changes how we see the world. It strips away our innocence and we grow up well before we should. It is as though I was walking along a similar path with these other girls and then we reached a fork in the road. I continued on my journey that included the experience of abuse and they continued on theirs. My path was a bit thornier, bleaker, but there were clearings at times where I could see the other path and the sun and laughter that was there. I would try to soak up as much of it as I could—if even from a distance—but could never seem to break away from the path I was on.

This universal experience of abuse survivors—of being forced to grow up too soon and, as a result, feeling like we just do not belong—is one that stays with us for a long time. **It is often one of our deepest stories—"I don't belong."**

As adults, we often find it hard to relate to others who have not shared our same path. We long for the look of recognition and ability to think deeply about things that matter and are turned off by relationships and conversations that remain shallow.

The trouble is that we are constantly out to prove that we do not belong. So, regardless of the situation, we stand on the outside and judge or evaluate rather than engage and bring an attitude of openness. We need to understand that the story of "I don't belong" greatly impacts how we connect to others. We may find it harder to connect with others, but we only exacerbate the problem when we continue to have the attitude that we are somehow an outsider, flawed, damaged, or never fit in.

We also need to accept and appreciate that not everyone is our cup of tea! It is okay if we do not connect with someone. Our job is to not use this as further evidence to support our story.

Reflection

How has loneliness been a part of your life?

_____

_____

_____

_____

What thoughts or self-talk do you have that make you feel lonely?
Example: Nobody likes me; no one understands me.

_____

_____

How do you isolate yourself from others?

_____

_____

What do you do when you are feeling lonely?

_____

_____

Have you ever felt like you belong? List some people, groups, or communities to which you belong?

_____

_____

_____

_____

Did you know that being lonely can actually provide us an opportunity for growth? Our ability to sit and remain grounded in the lonely times is no small thing. In *The Great Divorce*, C.S. Lewis is telling the story of a man who has lost his son and is experiencing a deep sense of loss and emptiness—loneliness. Lewis writes that, in this void, "in the loneliness, in the silence, something else might begin to grow." When I read this, it immediately jumped out at me. Lewis did not go on to explain what that "something else" was, but I think it is *independence*.

The experience of abuse often leaves us clamoring for love, affection, and attention. We bounce from relationship to relationship, job to job, activity to activity, refusing to ever stop long enough to deal with who we are when we are on our own. Now, this is in no way related to the popular idea that we must "love ourselves before we can love others." I think, quite frankly, that is a ridiculous statement. I have actually come to love myself much more deeply through the relationships and reflections of my partners than when I was on my own.

What we can gain by developing the capacity to be in the loneliness is a sense that we can stand on our own two feet. We come to understand that the love and experiences that come with being with others are amazing and to be appreciated, but **we also learn that our existence is not dependent upon "belonging."**

As a result, one very important thing changes: We stop saying "yes" to things just because we are afraid of being alone or trying to prove that we do belong. Instead, we begin to powerfully choose for ourselves who we want to spend time with and what experiences we want to have.

Furthermore, we can learn to appreciate the "happy people," as I call them. We may not enjoy spending a lot of one-on-one time with them, but we can, in fact, soak in their lightness, giggles, set aside our cares, and just enjoy the simple things with them.

Reflection

What things are you saying "yes" to out of the fear of being alone or not belonging?

_____

_____

What are the payoffs and costs of the story "I don't belong"?

_____

_____

_____

_____

Homework

Practice challenging the stories that cause you to feel lonely and disconnected. Also notice how your time alone changes when you use it as an opportunity to develop independence rather than as a chance to reinforce false beliefs (e.g., I will always be alone, I don't belong).

Bonus: Friendship in a time of casual acquaintances

"Friendship is more than acquaintance, and it involves more than affection. Friendship usually rises out of mutual interests and common aims, and these pursuits are strengthened by the benevolent impulses that sooner or later grow. The demands of friendship for frankness, for self-revelation, for taking friends' criticisms as seriously as their expressions of admiration or praise, for stand-by-me loyalty, and for assistance to the point of self-sacrifice are all potent encouragements to moral maturation and even ennoblement.

In our age, when casual acquaintance often comes so easily, and when intimacy comes too soon and too cheaply, we need to be reminded that genuine friendships take time. They take effort to make, and work to keep. Friendship is a deep thing."

—William J. Bennett

I find that so many of us—often with 400 social media "friends" or more—still feel like we have no deep human relationships. We can access each other in seconds and, perhaps because of this, have lost the stomach for enduring with each other through time and circumstance in order to form solid connections.

Additionally, we seem to cringe at the idea of committing to anything that takes more than half an hour, and so miss out on opportunities where friendships could flourish. For example, every time I mention that I dance with a hip-hop crew and we rehearse twice a week for two hours, mouths drop open, eyes glaze over, and people are amazed that I give so much of my time to "one thing!" Yet this time dedicated to a group of people and doing something that I love has resulted in real friendships. So, being willing to commit to one thing may actually prove to be more valuable than doing lots of different things.

I was particularly touched by Bennett's statement, because I am finding more and more that it is my "real" friends who have the most impact on my life, on who I am. My understanding of what it means to be a friend and to be befriended has grown exponentially since my twenties ... and, quite frankly, some days it is a challenge to remain accessible and tuned in.

But, overall, I am deeply grateful to those in my life who have found me worth their time, who have stayed with me through many adventures, who have made the "effort" to keep me, and are enjoying the journey with me.

It is also inspiring to think of the friendships that are yet to be formed—the unknown faces and lives that may pop into my life at any time and who will then look back in amazement with me years later that something so wonderful could have been born out of one simple moment!

Today, take a moment to thank your "real" friends—the people who you belong to—for loving you so unconditionally, for bailing you out, for setting you straight, for laughing and crying with you, and for seeing in you what you have a hard time seeing in yourself.

Lesson 23
Abandonment

Abandon: *to leave completely and finally, forsake utterly, desert, to give up, discontinue, withdraw from, withdraw protection or support*

When it comes to abandonment, we are very much driven by a fear of the unknown. We do not know if the people we are connecting to may one day withdraw their protection or support. They may "forsake" us, and not just a little, but *utterly*. The greater the connection, the greater the risk, because we have more at stake should the person choose to walk away.

In an effort to alleviate this terrible sense of "not knowing," we will often do a variety of things. We will over-control, seek constant reassurance, or be on high alert for anything that looks like withdrawal. Worst-case scenario, as soon as we start to feel close, we will push away and sabotage the relationship.

The fear of abandonment is extremely common in those of us who have been abused. We have experienced very real and tangible abandonment, the loss of protection by those who were supposed to care for us. Unfortunately, we then begin living as if this is going to be the case with everyone we come across.

For quite a long time, I had the false belief that "people always leave." As a result, guess what, people around me often didn't stick around for long, because I would pretty much act in a way that ensured they would not want to! It is hard to acknowledge, but we have to be straight about the role we play that leads us to re-create the experience of being abandoned over and over again.

Reflection

Who abandoned you and how did they abandon you?

_____

_____

_____

_____

What have you come to believe about people and relationships as a result?

_____

_____

_____

_____

What do you do to protect yourself from being abandoned? How do you behave?

_____

_____

_____

How do you contribute, if at all, to the cycle of abandonment?

_____

_____

_____

How do you cope with or try to manage your "fear of the unknown"?

_____

_____

_____

Earlier, I gave you just the first part of the definition of abandonment. Here is the rest:

To give up the control of, to yield (oneself) without restraint or moderation

When I read this, I thought, "Hmm, maybe I need to abandon myself to abandonment!" Our relationships can thrive if we are willing to shift our focus and energy away from trying to prevent the withdrawal of others and enter into an open, free space, where we are present to the fact that they are here with us right now, in this moment. Instead of maneuvering to try to get some guarantee that they will always be here no matter what, we can appreciate the person for being here right now.

The point is, that fear of abandonment keeps us so focused on the future "what ifs" that we miss out on what is happening right now. Another, and more tragic, outcome is that we behave so poorly as a result of our fear, that we pretty much guarantee that things will fall apart.

There is no getting away from taking risks in relationships. We can, however, learn to take *calculated* risks. This means we have to get out of the nasty habit of connecting to others who are so high risk that we are pretty much setting ourselves up for failure.

One client, intent on maneuvering to get some guarantee that his girlfriend would never leave, would text her every couple of hours to keep tabs on her. If he did not get an immediate response, his meaning making machine would immediately kick into gear, leading him to thoughts such as "She must be with someone else." As we worked together to challenge his false beliefs, he first had to acknowledge that, while it was *possible* that she was with someone else, it was *unlikely* given all of the experiences they had shared. Furthermore, her actions time and again indicated she was committed. The risk he was taking in trusting her therefore seemed well calculated. We then decided that he must hit the pause button (no meaning making) for four hours after sending a text and would limit his texting to three times a day. Over time, his fear and anxiety gradually abated and he was able to form a deeper bond based on trust and respect rather than fear and anxiety.

We need to practice giving up trying to control the future and remain in the present moment. We also need to give some thought to the types of risks we are taking—are they measured (even if still daring) or just playing with fire?

Reflection

How can you shift your focus from trying to control future outcomes to what is happening right now?

_____

_____

_____

How do you know if you are taking a calculated risk or not?

_____

_____

_____

_____

Finally, another type of abandonment is self-abandonment. Not caring for ourselves may show up by our not taking care of our physical health, being careless in relationships, not asking for what we need, or not setting boundaries.

How do you abandon yourself?

_____

_____

What steps can you take to begin caring for yourself?

_____

_____

_____

_____

Homework

Spend some time reflecting on and creating some strategies for grounding yourself in the present. You might use the exercise we learned in Lesson 20 to reduce your anxiety about the future "what ifs" by exploring how you would handle things if a relationship ended. You might develop a breathing exercise that helps ground you to the present moment. You might create a declaration—"All I have is this moment"—that you say when you find yourself drifting too far into the future. Whatever you choose, remember the goal is to withdraw your focus from "someday" and bring it back to "today."

PART 7
SHARING YOUR STORY

Lesson 24
Breaking the Silence

We have come a very long way in this journey of recovery, and I hope, by now, you have successfully identified some of the false beliefs that were created as a result of the abuse. I hope that you are using clear requests to communicate powerfully, that you are out proving some amazing and freeing things rather than reinforcing old ways of being, and that you are constantly creating new neuronal pathways by challenging your stories.

It is time now to break the silence. To tell your story. I like what Kubetin-Littlefield says in *Shelter from the Storm* about this process:

> *"To actually tell someone exactly what happened during the abuse is frightening. We can talk about the fact that we were abused and how we feel about the event, the perpetrator ... and still almost pretend it happened to someone else. When we write about and talk about the actual details, when and where it happened, and how we felt then and there, we take power over the shame and guilt. We have faced the event head-on. It is no longer chasing us. We have caught it and taken power over it. We have also broken through the power of the secret."*

I know this can be a bit confronting, but I have all the confidence in the world that you can do it. Especially since I am going to give you some guidance.

Reflection

How are you feeling about telling or writing your story?

_____

_____

If you are feeling resistance, what are some of the benefits of taking on this next step?

_____

_____

Part One

We are going to start by first thinking of the abuse **as a whole.** Set aside some time for this—it cannot be done in the five minutes before you need to pick the kids up from school! When you have made sure you have enough time (and someone on call for support should you need it), begin writing your answers to these questions (adapted from *Secret Survivors* by E. Sue Blume):

1. Describe what happened (recall the details of the abuse as a whole, big picture).

2. Describe how you felt at the time.

3. Describe how it has affected your life (remember its mark on your life to date).

4. Describe what you want from the abuser now.

Once you have completed the exercise above, you are ready for Part Two. I do not suggest completing Part One and Part Two on the same day, but you can do so if you are feeling safe and ready.

Part Two

We are now going to consider **one specific moment** from the abuse to write about.

1. Use your abuser's name as often as possible. If you do not know your abuser's name, just choose a label that you are comfortable with.

2. Think of a **specific** moment that occurred that is prominent in your mind or significant and write about that. Usually, if you just sit still, get quiet, that moment will pop into your mind. Describe what happened—just the facts.
   My example: My grandfather said, "Just let me play with you."

3. Next, consider what your interpretation was, what story was created in that moment, and write about that.
   My example: I am a toy, an object to be used by men.

4. Then look for the alternative explanations in order to create a new meaning.
   My example: My grandfather wanted to gain permission in order to alleviate his guilt.

5. Finally, create a declaration (statement of truth) that you can begin speaking in order to transform your thoughts and way of being.
   My example: I am not an object to be used. I am a beautiful woman and deserve to be treated with respect, gentleness, and adoration.

If you are completing this guidebook on your own, I want to encourage you to read what you have just written out loud to someone you trust. Make a clear request of the person, so they know exactly what you need (e.g., "I just want you to listen to this and then hug me when I'm finished"). If you do not have anyone, read it out loud to yourself. There is so much power in the spoken word; allowing yourself to tell your story using this specific model is a great experience.

You can always share your story with me! Email me at coach@rachelgrantcoaching.com or post your story by emailing beyondsurvivors@groups.facebook.com (this is a private group—only members will see your post).

You can return to this exercise to explore different moments of the abuse that occurred to discover the meanings and stories that were created at specific times. Then do the steps to challenge those meanings in order to chip away at the false beliefs that were wired in the past.

It is important to understand that telling your story should become a way of connecting to the moments when false beliefs were created rather than as an opportunity to rehash the past. Every time you tell your story (to yourself or others), include all of the pieces—what happened, your interpretation, your alternative explanation, and your declaration. By doing this, you are challenging your old wiring connected to the experience and reinforcing your new understanding.

The more you do this, the less scary it is to say, "I was abused," because you will be ready to express it as something that happened with insights into how it has shaped who you are minus the shame, fear, embarrassment, or emotional upset that you have likely experienced when talking about the abuse previously.

Homework

Treat yourself to something nice after you complete this process—you deserve it!

PART 8
RELATIONSHIPS

Lesson 25
Family Matters

We are now going to turn our attention to the relationships that played such an important part in shaping who we are—family. In my opinion, growing up in a family where abuse is occurring is one of the most difficult things a person can face. Even if our abuser is outside of the family, the way in which our family responds to the abuse is fundamental to how we are able to cope and heal.

Furthermore, it is no easy thing for a parent to find out that their child has been abused, let alone if the abuse is at the hands of their own spouse or family member. This is not to let them off the hook if their responses were less than supportive or, at worst, if they outright did not believe us. It is simply an effort to acknowledge that abuse convolutes the roles and relationships for each family member.

Did you tell anyone in your family about the abuse? If so, who did you talk to and when?

_____

_____

How did your family members respond to the abuse?

_____

_____

Did a family member ever share with you that they had been abused? What impact did this have on you?

_____

_____

Let's take a look at what kind of family culture you grew up in. **Check off any of the following that apply to your family** (adapted from *Shelter from the Storm*).

- ☐ Needy family members receive an inappropriate proportion of the family's time, attention, and energy. Members learn to be overly responsible for others and neglect themselves.
- ☐ Denial and secrecy are encouraged.
- ☐ Emotions are repressed, explosive, or both.
- ☐ Children are not taught effective living and relationship skills. Children do not learn to touch, feel, or trust. They learn to expect emotional or physical abandonment.
- ☐ Members are squeezed into rigid, inappropriate roles.
- ☐ Other: _____

Of the characteristics you checked off, which ones are still present in your family today?

_____

_____

The last item on the list above refers to the fact that children in families where abuse occurs generally develop survival roles. These roles are either assigned or unconsciously chosen by the child.

Some examples of survival roles include (from *Shelter from the Storm*):

- **Scapegoat**: Usually blamed for family problems
- **Hero**: Works hard to bring respect to the family name
- **Surrogate Spouse**: Often takes the place of the emotionally absent spouse and becomes the child counselor for a troubled adult parent
- **Lost Child**: Never gets in the way or causes trouble because this family has enough problems
- **Surrogate Parent**: Takes over responsibility of parenting tasks
- **Clown**: Avoids the pain by being the center of attention

Which survival role(s) were you assigned or did you choose? Feel free to identify a role not listed above.

_____

_____

How did this role help you cope with the abuse?

_____

_____

What roles did other family members play?

_____

_____

We often find that, as soon as we are around our family members, we fall right back into old patterns of relating and being. It's kinda like how my Oklahoma accent really shows up as soon as I am around my mom! Also, whatever role we played in our family, we likely still get caught up in playing that same role today in other areas of our life.

How are you continuing to play this role and in which relationships or what areas of life?

_____

_____

For clients or course participants: What role are you playing in our course or coaching relationship?

_____

_____

In addition to the roles we take on in the family and later continue playing, there are some core false beliefs that develop for people who grow up in families where abuse occurred.

Let's spend some time exploring these (adapted from *Shelter from the Storm*).

I must meet certain standards in order to feel good about myself.

What standards must you meet in order to believe you are a good person? Focus on the standards that are getting in the way of your recovery.

Example: In order to feel good about myself, I must never make mistakes, I must hide my feelings.

_____

_____

I must have the approval of others.

In what ways do you sacrifice your own integrity or authenticity when seeking the approval of others?

Example: I won't speak up when I disagree, because I am afraid others will be upset.

_____

_____

Because I have failed, I am unworthy and deserve to be punished.

What are you still punishing yourself for?

Example: I was not strong enough to stand up to my abuser.

_____

_____

I am what I am. I cannot change—I am hopeless.

What things do you most believe are unchangeable or cause you to be hopeless?

Example: No one seems to think I can change; I cannot control my anger.

_____

_____

One important thing to understand here is that there is nothing, in general, wrong with having standards or needing approval. Problems occur, however, when we set up these beliefs as "musts." If, for example, we cannot function or feel good about ourselves without the approval of others, then things have gotten out of balance. The work to be done is to find ways to balance these needs.

Rewrite the false beliefs above as new stories that will give you freedom, possibility, and balance.

Example: I can feel good about myself even when I make a mistake, because it means I am trying and learning.

_____

_____

_____

_____

Much of who we are and how we see the world is shaped by the family we grew up in. We received all sorts of messages about what behavior was and was not acceptable. At times, family members may have made statements that influenced how we saw ourselves, relationships, or the world. The thing is, whatever messages our family members gave us are simply that—messages, opinions, or their perceptions. We can now begin to make choices about which of these messages we will and will not allow to shape how we see and experience the world today.

What messages about yourself did you get from your family?

Example: I'll never be good enough.

_____

_____

_____

_____

What messages about relationships did you get from your family?

_____

_____

_____

_____

What messages do you want to let go of or no longer be shaped by?

_____

_____

_____

_____

Finally, the more we reinforce these messages or play these roles in our families, relationships, the more we reinforce certain ways of being. When we have it that we "are" the clown, the loyal daughter, the scapegoat, the black sheep of the family, the outsider, the child-parent, the achiever, **we remain trapped with no possibilities, because we frame all of our behavior using this lens and tend to limit ourselves to a particular way of being based on the role we believe we have to play.**

What role have you decided that you have to play in life? How do you define yourself?
Example: I am the practical one; I am the dependable one; I am the caregiver; I am the screw-up; I am the leader.

_____

_____

_____

A client who played the surrogate spouse role and whose way of being was "the dependable one" constantly set aside her own needs and plans whenever her mother would call on her. She was so attached to being reliable that she was unable to set healthy boundaries. As we worked together, she first began challenging this way of being by setting clearer boundaries (e.g., I am only available on Fridays to help you run errands). What she eventually came to understand was, now that she was helping out of a genuine desire rather than as obligated by a way of being, she actually enjoyed the time spent with her mother. Additionally, because she wasn't sacrificing her own needs and desires, she no longer resented her mother for asking for support. As an added bonus, her mother began reaching out to others for support, so also broke out of the pattern of seeing her daughter as "the dependable" one and perhaps herself as "the needy one."

These defined roles (ways of being) limit who we get to be for ourselves and others, keeping relationships superficial and limited.

What are the costs given how you define yourself?

_____

_____

_____

What would become possible if you gave up this way of being, playing this role?

_____

_____

_____

The next, and often harder, level has to do with the people in our lives. Notice that we tend to use our experiences with others to determine—or prove—things about them. We begin to define who they "are." For example, my mother is overbearing, my father is cold and disconnected, or my husband is lazy. When we have it that someone else "is" the provider, the dependable one, the loser, the aggressor, this keeps us and them trapped with no possibility, because we frame all of their behavior with this lens or limit them to a particular way of being.

What do you have the people in your life being? How do you define them?

Example: My mother is a nuisance. My father is the one I can trust. My husband is my life.

_____

_____

_____

_____

What are the costs of how you are defining others?

Example: If my husband is my life, I am not owning and taking responsibility for my own journey.

_____

_____

What new possibilities become available by giving up who you have them being?

Example: If I give up defining my husband as my life, I'll experience independence and relieve him of the enormous pressure of being "my life"!

_____

_____

When we determine who others will be, we limit and suffocate them and harm ourselves in the process, because we are unable to embrace the entire person. If our abuser is still in our life, one of the hardest but most freeing steps we can take at this point is to stop defining them as "the abuser" and to begin seeing the whole person. Being able to broaden our perspective by embracing and acknowledging that this person *was* an abuser and also *is* my father, mother, friend, etc. creates room for connection and new possibilities for relating. This is particularly important if we desire any sort of real relationship to occur.

Homework

Go to three people who matter to you and share with them who you have had them being and what you now see as possible because you are giving that up.

Steps:

1. Tell the person how you have been defining them.

2. Share the cost.

3. Create a new possibility.

Example: Mom, I've been thinking about our relationship, and I noticed that I have come to think that you are always on my brother's side when we disagree about something. It's like I think you are my enemy in some way. I realize that believing this is causing me to feel anxious and defensive when we are together and to not share myself with you. I see that I need to let that go and would like to share more of myself with you. Maybe we could meet up for lunch once a week.

Also spend some time paying attention to your own ways of being. Which ways of being are you choosing and which ones are present out of obligation or as a result of a false belief?

Lesson 26
Trust

Many survivors struggle with trust. It is not surprising given that our fundamental trust in another person was shattered as a result of abuse. In fact, it is hard for some survivors to remember ever trusting anyone.

When I first thought about trusting others, I felt a huge knot in my stomach. I did not want to rely on the integrity or character of another person. After all, I had relied on the character of someone, and he abused me. I also had a very hard time believing that people would not always leave, let me down, or harm me. I was in a terrible loop of being out to prove that no one could be trusted, and I was succeeding.

There are a couple of layers involved when we think about trust: defining trust, trusting ourselves, trusting others and determining who is trustworthy, and, the biggie, embracing vulnerability (don't worry, we will take that on in the next lesson). So, we have a lot of work to do. Let's get started!

Reflection

Can you relate to the statement, "… it is hard for some survivors to remember ever trusting anyone"?

_____

_____

_____

_____

Who has violated your trust?

_____

_____

What has been the impact on your life of not being able to trust others?

_____

_____

_____

For me, the impact of not trusting others was that I walked around guarded all of the time. It was as if I was operating behind a piece of gauze; I remained fuzzy to others and others remained fuzzy to me. I was never able to experience real connection or intimacy.

To move you along toward breaking out from behind your walls, veils, protections, let's start by simply exploring what it is you think it means to trust someone in the first place.

Write your own definition of trust:

_____

_____

As we think about trust, we often focus on determining if a person is trustworthy or not. To be sure, this is very important. However, **trusting *yourself* is actually the first step!** If you do not have the confidence that you can make good decisions, judge others with wisdom and clarity, and set the boundaries that are necessary when others violate your trust, then thinking about trusting others will prove to be an empty and meaningless endeavor.

Reflection

On a scale of 1-10 (1 = never; 10 = too easily), how would you rate your ability to trust yourself?
_____

In what areas of life do you trust yourself to make good choices?

_____

_____

In what areas of life do you doubt your ability to make good choices?

_____

_____

I do not trust myself because ...

_____

_____

_____

_____

Too often we strive to be open to others, to trust, but find ourselves pulling away, making a mess of things, or being hurt by our choices. If you find yourself over and over again struggling to trust others, it is possible that your focus needs to be shifted from outward interactions to inward reflection and growth.

Being grounded in who you are, confident in your ability to make good decisions, and able to set and keep boundaries are critical components of trusting others.

Once we identify the beliefs that are holding us back from trusting ourselves, we need to do the work to challenge these beliefs. As in all things, start small. Setting a goal that focuses on just one area where you want to begin learning to trust yourself is a good place to begin.

I will begin trusting myself today by ...

_____

_____

Let's turn our attention now to trusting others. You may still have some work to do to trust yourself, but there is no time like the present to begin transforming your relationships.

On a scale of 1-10 (1 = never; 10 = too easily), how would you rate your ability to trust others?

_____

I cannot trust others, because ...

_____

_____

_____

To develop an ability to trust others, we must learn how to determine who is trustworthy. One of the biggest mistakes we make when determining who is trustworthy is looking for the qualities in others that we ourselves lack. Consider, for example, that we have a very hard time getting projects done on time. This is a quality that we would say a trustworthy person would possess. So, when working with others on a team, we label the woman who is able to get things done on time as trustworthy. Nevermind the fact that she cheats on her taxes. The point is we are so focused on the qualities that we lack that we misjudge the trustworthiness of another person whenever they possess those qualities.

Reflection

What do you look for in others that you feel you lack yourself?

_____

_____

_____

What guidelines do you usually use to determine if someone is trustworthy?

_____

_____

_____

Do you think your guidelines are so strict that they keep everyone out or are they too loose and let everyone in?

_____

_____

_____

As a result of abuse, our "trust meter" is a bit off balance. We have it tilted way over to not trusting, trusting too easily, or remain apathetic about it, never really connecting or pushing away others. So, how can we give our trust meter a tune-up and rebalance it?

First, we need to challenge our general understanding of what trust is. Regardless of what you have thought it means, I want you to try on a new understanding of trust.

- Trust is not about judging the character and quality of another person.
- We do not come to trust a person as a whole.
- Rather, we come to trust the person to honor a specific commitment.
- No one is 100 percent trustworthy.

Remember the example of the team member who finishes her work on time, but cheats on her taxes? She is completely trustworthy when it comes to completing tasks on time. She is not trustworthy when it comes to dealing with the IRS. For any given person, there is always some commitment we can trust, but there is always another we cannot. This is why **trust is not about judging the character or quality of a person, but rather judging and evaluating the commitments you can trust the person to honor.**

When relating to others, we should seek to know the difference between commitments likely to be honored and those that likely will not. We want to understand what sorts of commitments a person follows through on more often than not and hope that these line up with what is important to us. This will vary by person and by commitment.

Our job then is to decide whether or not to trust someone by considering their behavior and speech as signals of their beliefs, values, and intentions, which are all indications of what commitments they are willing to keep, how often, and for how long. Keep in mind that behavior is a much better indicator than what people say.

Let's bring this all together with a familiar example: the friend who always cancels at the last minute.

> You have just begun a new friendship with Greg and he seems like a great guy. Friendly, down-to-earth, smart, and the two of you just seem to click. You have gone out a few times and really enjoyed yourselves, that is, when he manages to show up. Though Greg said he was really looking forward to dinner tonight, he just texted to say he can't make it. This is about the fifth time this has happened.

> Can you trust Greg to keep his commitment to show up for events? Nope.

> Can you trust Greg to be present, fun, and enjoyable when you are together? Yes.

Can you trust Greg overall? It depends on what you value more. No one is 100 percent trustworthy, but the scale can tip in one direction or the other. For one person, Greg canceling is in such contradiction to their own values that the scale tips toward untrustworthy. For another person, the quality of the time they have when they are together is more important, and so the scale tips in the other direction toward trustworthy.

Moreover, we must come to understand that trust is not an all-or-nothing deal. We can trust someone in a few minor ways and still enjoy them. We may have others in our lives who we trust more deeply and for a greater number of things. It is important to move away from the trap of thinking that each person in our life must be trusted at the same level.

Once we have developed a healthy trust meter, we will be able to determine where someone falls on this spectrum based on which commitments we come to believe they will keep and relate to them accordingly.

Oh, and the bad news is …

In case you missed it, there is no such thing as a 100 percent trustworthy person, which means there is no guarantee that people will not let us down, hurt us, or behave terribly.

But, the good news is …

We do not have to judge the person as a whole and give them a badge of trustworthy honor. Instead, we can prioritize our beliefs, values, and intentions, and judge to see if the person can commit to those things.

You see, trusting another person is not about saying "You're good, you're safe"—it is about saying "I know that, in these areas, I can count on you, and I acknowledge and understand the areas where I can't." If we continue striving to prove that someone is "good," then, as soon as they show a flaw, we will cut them off, deem them untrustworthy, and continue our cycle of being closed off and disconnected.

By the way, this also applies when thinking about our own commitments and trustworthiness!

Reflection

I can trust myself to keep my commitments to ... even if I am unable to commit in other ways:

_____

_____

_____

_____

I can trust a person if they keep their commitments to ... even if they are unable to commit in other ways:

_____

_____

_____

_____

Homework

Are there commitments that you have given your word to that you have not followed through on—either to yourself or others? Write about this and reflect upon the impact this is having on yourself or others.

Are there commitments that matter to you that someone close to you is not keeping? What is the impact on the relationship? Have you talked to the person about your feelings? Write about this and reflect upon the impact if you have not communicated with the person or if you have not set a boundary in this area.

Lesson 27
Vulnerability

"Any sign of weakness or vulnerability is unthinkable. If others discover we are weak, they will have power over us and this knowledge will be used against us."

—Cynthia Kubetin-Littlefield, *Shelter from the Storm*

Life after abuse feels like a battlefield. We become like warriors, constantly striving to guard ourselves from being wounded or hurt again. In fact, by definition, being vulnerable means to be capable of or susceptible to being wounded or hurt. Is it any wonder that we resist vulnerability with such adamant force?

We have experienced very real moments when our weakness, naivety, lack of control or power was fully used against us. Once we escaped the abuse, we became determined to never be used or harmed in such a way again.

In addition, we lost all sense of safety and security, which needs to be present in order to embrace vulnerability. In an effort to regain a sense of safety and security, we typically abandon vulnerability and instead focus on being controlling. Same song, different day, right?

Our need to be in control of outcomes drives so many of our behaviors. This, however, is where we make the greatest error in recovery. Being controlling only provides a false sense of security—an illusion! Whereas, through the openness and sensitivity that vulnerability requires, we develop deeper and stronger connections that can be relied upon and trusted with greater confidence.

It is a huge false belief to think that we can actually prevent or avoid vulnerability. All of us, no matter what we do, are capable of being physically or emotionally wounded. There is no escaping vulnerability, so we might as well embrace it and use it to our own benefit.

But how?

First, we need to identify and challenge the false beliefs that we have developed around vulnerability. You can start by answering these questions:

If I am vulnerable, it means that ...

_____

_____

When I consider being vulnerable, I think or feel ...

_____

_____

Next, to be exposed (vulnerable) means to be open and susceptible to harm. But, it also means that we will be open and susceptible to many wonderful things as well!

What are the good things you become open to or gain access to by being vulnerable?

_____

_____

I am not advocating that we let down the drawbridge for just anyone, but I am asking that we at least remove the rusted chains and locks so that we can invite others in when the time comes in order to experience those things you just identified as benefits of vulnerability.

Thirdly, it is important that we consider who and what we are opening ourselves up to. Many of our fears of and beliefs about being vulnerable (e.g., to need another person means to be powerless) have been reinforced by our own bad choices regarding who we open ourselves up to. Now, we do not need to feel guilty or ashamed about that, but we do need to understand that **openness and vulnerability may not actually be the culprits here**. The real problem may be who or what we are choosing to be open to and our poor evaluation of the risks involved.

A new skill to develop then is the ability to better evaluate and control the risks involved, which I want to distinguish from "being controlling." The former involves evaluating a situation and others and considering how we might *manage or reduce* the risk. The latter involves trying to manipulate or change a person or circumstances so as to *eliminate* all risk. Essentially, it is the difference between being "in control" and "being controlling."

Reflection

How have you avoided being vulnerable and instead used being controlling to gain a sense of safety and security in your relationships?

Example: I always want to decide what we are going to do and when.

_____

_____

_____

In your body?

Example: I refuse to eat in a healthy way or I have to follow a very strict diet.

_____

_____

_____

In your circumstances?

Example: Everything must go as planned. I don't like being caught off-guard.

_____

_____

_____

In your environment?

Example: My house must be clean and orderly—nothing out of its place.

_____

_____

_____

What is the impact on you or others as a result of avoiding vulnerability and instead being controlling?

Example: There is tension, distrust, and a lack of connection. I have a false sense of security.

_____

_____

What choices have you been making, risks have you been taking, that reinforce your false beliefs about vulnerability?

Example: I always date married women.

_____

_____

How might you begin managing risks (be in control) rather than trying to eliminate them (being controlling)?

Note: Managing risks involves focusing on your own choices and behaviors—not on the other person.

_____

_____

Finally, we need to understand, I mean really understand, that there is always a risk involved in everything we do and in every relationship. But, without risk, there is no reward. Check out this additional definition of vulnerability in the context of a bridge game:

> *"liable to increased penalties but* **entitled to increased bonuses** *after winning a game in contract bridge"*

> —Merriam-Webster Dictionary

I love that! To be vulnerable in this card game means that we will likely experience penalties but we are also promised increased bonuses after winning. In the game of Beyond Surviving, to be vulnerable means that we will likely experience disappointments and hurts—there is a risk—but we are also entitled to payoffs. These include intimacy, connection, adventure, authenticity, joy, and independence—lots of bonuses!

Homework

Pick out an area of life where you are over-controlling. What would it be like to give up being controlling and instead embrace vulnerability? What steps would you need to take to let down your drawbridge? How will you manage the risks?

For an additional perspective on vulnerability, watch **"The Power of Vulnerability"** (Track 6).

Bonus: The payoff of vulnerability

I have had friends say to me from time to time, "Things just seem to flow for you. Jobs, relationships—they just seem to come to you ... why is that?" I have never really been able to answer this question well, but, as I reflected upon this concept of "flow," I was reminded of a moment that taught me a lot about vulnerability. I will give you the punch line first and then tell all the dirty details. I lost my job one day and got hired for a new job the next day!

Now let's go back in time:

While I was still working as a mentor for teens in 2009, each leader was asked to write up a personal profile that would be shared with the parents and teens. One of the questions was: What are your dreams and aspirations? Now, the typical responses were often about wanting to start a family, some career goal, or places to travel. While I surely have some similar intentions for my life (Italy!), when I thought about what I really dream and aspire to be and do, I realized my answer would not fit the status quo. So, now, a decision presented itself: Go with the standard response or be authentic?

Here is what I wrote:

> *"To live in such a way that people are better off for having known me. To love unconditionally, to forgive radically, and to live with integrity."*

Now, those thoughts are so key to who I am that putting them out there for just anyone to see was stepping into being vulnerable and giving up being stingy with myself by sharing. It also meant risking being misunderstood or judged.

A week after the profiles were posted, I got a call from a mom who had seen the posting. She said, "I read that and immediately knew you were someone I needed to connect with!" We had an hour-long conversation, getting to know each other. She shared with me that her company produced and distributed meal replacement products. I had no interest in becoming a "salesperson," but I filed the information away as something to keep in mind for others.

The day after I lost my job, I called her, because I had some extra cash (read "severance package") and wanted to give her products a try. The conversation began by her asking the usual "How are things going?" Rather than give the standard answer of "Fine," I said, "Well, it's been an interesting week! Yesterday ..." and I went on to explain what happened with my job. I also decided to share about a possible tutoring opportunity I had lined up. To which she said, "Oh, I've been looking for a tutor for my daughter! How about I hire you?!" ... and there ya go! ... I had a new source of income. On top of that, because she knew my situation, she offered to work with me on the cost of her products, so I could go ahead and give them a try!

As I smile again at remembering how one door closes and another door opens, I have decided that the flow in my life is directly related to:

1. A willingness to give up looking good, to be authentic, to be genuine about myself, my life, my needs, and my desires as often as possible even when doing so goes against social norms or what feels most comfortable.

2. By living authentically, I get into communication with people and share in a way that is vulnerable, open, and non-stingy.

3. This creates the space for opportunities and support from others to flow into my life either from the person directly or from someone whom they may know.

If you were to set aside looking good, the fear of being vulnerable (or whatever else it is that stops you), what would you do today? Who would you get in touch with? What phone call would you make that you have been putting off?

_____

_____

_____

_____

_____

_____

Lesson 28
Intimacy

One of the biggest payoffs of learning to trust (ourselves and others) and of embracing vulnerability is intimacy, which is something we need and crave.

Underline the phrase or phrases that describe your need for intimacy (adapted from *Shelter from the Storm*):

Afraid of it

Open and ready

Don't want it

Starving to death for it

What is it?

Too painful

Impossible

Don't know how to get it

Why risk it?

Overwhelming

Terrifying

Other _____

Before we delve into the work of identifying the reasons why we avoid intimacy and how to break free of the patterns that are keeping us from experiencing all of the goodness that comes from intimate relationships, let's spend some time considering what intimacy is. After all, if we do not know what it is, how will we know when we have it?

Reflection

Write your own definition of intimacy:

_____

_____

What sorts of actions, words, and behaviors feel like intimacy to you?

_____

_____

_____

I once came across this definition of intimacy that I really liked:

> *"Private and personal knowledge detailed and obtained by much study or experience"*

Intimacy involves both the ability to give and receive love and grows over time as we have experiences with or "study" the person we are connecting with. One of the main problems we experience having been abused, however, is that we tend to jump ship well before any of that can happen. Thus, our relationships remain superficial, never delving into detailed private and personal sharing. Why is that? Why do we avoid intimacy like it is the plague?

Many of the topics we have explored play a major role in our inability to both give and receive love intimately—distrust, betrayal, fear, guilt, shame, just to name a few. Hopefully, by now, you are beginning to gain a sense of freedom from these.

In addition, we have a whole host of fears and false beliefs that need to be challenged and unraveled in order to break free from the isolation that occurs when we avoid intimacy.

Mark the following statements T (true) or F (false) (from *Shelter from the Storm*):

- ☐ Intimacy means that we blindly trust people.
- ☐ Intimacy means physical or emotional isolation.
- ☐ Intimacy means betrayal.
- ☐ Intimacy means agreeing with another person when you know that person is not right.
- ☐ Intimacy means disclosing private or personal information when you do not want or wish to.
- ☐ Intimacy means abuse.

What other false beliefs do you have about intimacy?

_____

_____

_____

As a result of these false beliefs, we may try to avoid or detach from our need for intimacy. This often causes us to compensate in some way. Review the list below and mark any of the behaviors that you use to avoid intimacy and describe how this shows up in your life (adapted from *Shelter from the Storm*):

____ Substituting

Example: perfectionism, false compassion, attention demanding behavior.

_____

_____

____ Compulsive Behaviors

Example: eating, smoking, shopping, sex, work, religion, TV.

_____

_____

____ Suppressing the Need

_____

_____

____ Fantasy

_____

_____

____ Self-Pity

_____

_____

___ Anger

_____

_____

___ Unforgiveness/Rigidity

_____

_____

___ A Judgmental Attitude

_____

_____

___ Over-scheduling

(See the section "Overwhelmed by Choices?" below for more info on this very common behavior.)

_____

_____

What other ways do you avoid intimacy?

_____

_____

We engage in all of these behaviors because we are trying to avoid the loss that comes when intimate relationships end or because of the false beliefs we have about what comes along with intimacy. Answer the next question:

By never entering into intimate relationships, I get to avoid …

_____

_____

_____

_____

But consider this: Any behavior we use to avoid losing actually causes us to lose! We have seen time and again the costs of trying to outrun or ignore any of our basic human needs. Answer this question:

By never entering into intimate relationships, I never get to experience ...

_____

_____

_____

_____

One of the biggest reasons we avoid intimate relationships is that we ourselves do not know how to engage in a healthy way. We either isolate ourselves or become possessive or smothering should we connect with someone.

One client who had been married for years expressed his desire to experience deeper intimacy with his wife. He realized that he had withdrawn in many ways. In particular, he had stopped sharing with her any details about his day. He would arrive home, say a few passing words, and then retreat to his office. After identifying his false belief—"If I share myself too much, she will grow bored and leave"—we then put into place some strategies for challenging this false belief (e.g., right speech). He also took on the challenge of having a fifteen-minute conversation as soon as he arrived home. He discovered that these conversations would often turn into an hour or two, and he felt a growing sense of connection and understanding. Furthermore, his wife was ecstatic. He came to understand that his isolating behavior was not only harming him, it was also harming his wife.

Remember that intimacy includes the ability to both give and receive love. If we are isolating ourselves from others, there is no opportunity for an exchange. If we are possessive and smothering, then we are stuck in a mode of only taking and not giving. Our needs are center stage and the other person is being held accountable to make sure that we are constantly reassured, comforted, and paid attention to.

Furthermore, if we are engaging in any of these behaviors, we are also, once again, on the control wagon! By either managing ourselves or others, we are hoping to eliminate the risks that come along with intimacy.

Rather than repeat myself here, what do you imagine I would say to you about this controlling behavior?

_____

_____

By now, you may have noticed I have not mentioned sexual intimacy at all in this lesson. That is because intimacy, true intimacy, exists regardless of whether there is a sexual relationship or not. For too long, many of us have turned to sex as a substitute for intimacy, and we have been missing the boat on what real private and personal knowledge detailed and obtained by much study or experience is all about.

Don't worry though—we will get to sex in the next lesson!

If you checked off over-scheduling as one of your ways of avoiding intimacy, I encourage you to read the following section. If not, you can skip to Homework.

Overwhelmed by Choices?

"Although people believe they like to have lots of choices, in fact, having too many choices can be discouraging. Instead of making people feel more satisfied, a wide range of options can paralyze them. Studies show that when faced with two dozen varieties of jam in a grocery store, for example, or lots of investment options for their pension plan, people often choose arbitrarily or walk away without making any choice at all, rather than labor to make a reasoned choice."

—Gretchen Rubin, *The Happiness Project*

I suppose this isn't too shocking of an idea. I have also found myself staring blankly at a wall of canned soup. Wanting just a bit of chicken noodle, but being confronted with such variety, I abandon the purchase altogether and wander over to the bread aisle where … well, I didn't have much success there either.

I won't comment on how we got to the "more is better" way of thinking; I doubt I could say anything very new on that topic. What I will say is that this comment had me thinking about the many things I do have in my life to choose from and whether or not limiting my choices in one or more area might make a difference in the area of intimacy.

To my surprise, the first thing that popped into my mind was cutting back on the number of Meetup interest groups I am a part of. Upon closer examination, I noticed I had joined a ton of Meetup groups solely because they sounded like something I *should* be doing. Yet for all of my good intentions, I spent way more time deleting the invitation emails than actually attending any of the events!

So, I picked my top three and left all of the others, with some minor cringes of pain when saying goodbye to the karaoke, kayaking, and knitting groups (hmm … I swear there were non-"k" groups that got booted, too!). Giving up these groups did feel a bit like a loss—after all, shouldn't I want to be out in the world, doing new things, meeting new people? Yet at the end of the day, I had only created a clutter of choices for myself and was ending up on my couch watching TV anyway.

After trimming down my choices, I actually feel like I have more to do. I can say yes to each of my three groups consistently, because I am not spread so thin between twenty groups. Not surprisingly, the quality of the relationships I am forming in those groups is also improving. Fewer events have led to more, not less, connection and intimacy!

Amazingly enough, I went through this process with a client who had too many dates from which to choose. She felt like she was floundering in a sea of choices and was deathly afraid of making the wrong choice. So, she went silent and stopped responding to the men altogether. We worked through her fears of choosing, developed criteria for when to say "yes" and when to say "no," and winnowed down her options. She had some great dates, but, best of all, she felt better about her ability to not get stuck when too many options were available.

What could you do with a little less of in order to create more opportunities for intimacy?

Homework

Create an "Intimacy Is …" collage. You can go whole hog and whip out magazines, glue stick, and construction paper, or you can create a spreadsheet. The important thing is that you spend some time reflecting on what you would like to know and believe about intimacy, e.g., Intimacy is a walk on the beach, adventure, a risk worth taking, pillow talk.

Bonus: Some personal thoughts on intimacy

Now working on another year of life, I can say that I am better today than I was years, days, and hours ago. Yes, even hours, because each moment of life presents its own unique opportunity.

We make choices not every day, but every hour and every minute. Life can change in a split second. That is how long it takes to make a choice. Am I going to be loving or hateful, am I going to shout or speak softly, am I going to be open or closed off?

Humans desire simple things—love, respect, and friendship—but we are stubborn. We refuse to give before we receive—I want mine before I will give you yours. But in the very next moment, the person is no longer there to receive and what we had to give is now worthless. So why hold back the love we are naturally driven to express?

What is amazing to me is that, in those split-second moments, years are determined. Be mindful of your moments. Welcome love into each breath. Look, gaze adoringly on the ones you love, because, in the very next minute, they may no longer be standing before you.

Lesson 29
Say Yes to Sex

We have just spent time exploring vulnerability and intimacy, and one of the biggest payoffs of breaking out of our stories and patterns in these areas is that we move one step closer to being able to say "yes" to sex!

First of all, let's not be too bashful. Sex is a huge part of our lives. There is no getting around that, so we need to let go of any hang-ups or concerns we might have regarding talking about, exploring, or understanding sex.

Reflection

How comfortable are you talking about sex? If this is a hard topic for you, what would help or make it easier for you to discuss?

_____

_____

What messages were you given or lessons did you learn about talking about sex growing up?

_____

_____

Even if you are feeling a bit gun-shy about this topic, I encourage you to work through the lesson at your own pace, but do work through it. Trust me, the costs of not doing so are huge. So, let's get started!

In Lesson 12, you identified the types of abuse you experienced, which covered the whole spectrum—from the physical, to the visual, to the verbal. Even if we were never physically touched, our understanding of and relationship to sex was changed as a result of the abuse.

Below is a list of common responses to sex or sexual behaviors (adapted from *Shelter from the Storm*) that show up for people who have been abused. **Check off the ones that apply to you:**

- ☐ Unable to enjoy kissing
- ☐ Guilty or dirty feelings after sex or about sex
- ☐ Difficulty setting boundaries in sex
- ☐ Feeling guilty about the things you find pleasurable
- ☐ Inability to tolerate own body
- ☐ Dissociation from own body during sex
- ☐ Feeling of worthlessness if unable to provide sex
- ☐ Inability to look at a naked man or woman
- ☐ Phobic avoidance of genitals
- ☐ Effort to make life better with sex
- ☐ Avoidance of sexual activity
- ☐ Compulsive sexual behavior
- ☐ Sexual acting out
- ☐ Lack of sexual desire
- ☐ Feeling of being caught during sex
- ☐ Fear of letting go during sex or stopping yourself from feeling pleasure
- ☐ Crying during or after sex
- ☐ Feeling of being good only for sex
- ☐ Lack of sensitivity in a part of your body
- ☐ Difficulty with or inability to achieve orgasm
- ☐ Inability to have drug- or alcohol-free sex
- ☐ Desire to make partner responsible for sex
- ☐ Preoccupation with other concerns during sex
- ☐ Eagerness for sex to be over
- ☐ Feeling of having to perform during sex
- ☐ Inability to ask for sexual needs to be met
- ☐ Anger during or after sex
- ☐ Aversion to touching oneself
- ☐ Inability to be playful during sex
- ☐ Very strict rules for how sex should be

What other, if any, responses to sex or sexual behaviors do you have?

_____

_____

Some of these responses and behaviors may require the help of a trained therapist to overcome (e.g., dissociation). Yet the majority are the outcome of one very powerful false belief, "If sex did not exist, I wouldn't be in this mess in the first place!" In short, sex is bad. **The critical error here is that we are blaming sex instead of the abuser for what happened**.

As a result, we continue to connect what we experienced at the hands of our abuser with the experiences we are now having as adults. The touch of a lover is experienced as if it is the touch of the abuser. Words of seduction seem to be spoken in the same voice as the abuser.

However, there is a huge difference between our abuser and our lover, and a huge difference between the sex that occurred with the abuser and the sex that is occurring with our lover. The first step to take toward reclaiming our sex life is to distinguish or separate the sex that occurred during the abuse from the sex of our adult life. Let's explore this a bit more:

When you were abused, you were having sex out of ...

Example: Fear, obligation, forced submission

_____

_____

One very major thing was missing: consent. Our abuser never gave us a choice; sex occurred out of obligation and service to the abuser's desires. However, it is an error to continue thinking of sex as something we have to do or should do, that it is all about the other person, that we have no choice about it. We are adults now and we have the right to choose!

Right now, we might be choosing to avoid sex, hate sex, or fake enjoyment of sex. Yet we have the opportunity and the right to make different choices. Our lovers are not our abuser(s). We do not have to have sex with them out of obligation or for the sole purpose of meeting their needs.

If there is a part of our body that we do not like to have touched, we can ask our lover not to touch us there. Or we can choose to separate the touch that is occurring now from the touch that occurred then and give up the error of thinking that it is all the same!

Furthermore, we need to give up the lie that our sexual preferences are a result of abuse and therefore dysfunctional. If you like kinky sex, then this is what you prefer. If you like quiet, slow sex, then this is what you prefer. If you are a straight man who enjoys fantasizing about men, then this is what you prefer.

It is your choice. Period.

Reflection

What do you think the costs are of not reclaiming your sex life?

_____

_____

_____

_____

What choices are you making about sex?

_____

_____

_____

_____

What choices would you like to make instead?

_____

_____

_____

_____

At this time, sex for me is ...

_____

_____

I want sex to be ...

_____

_____

What is something you have always wanted to try, to say "yes" to?

_____

_____

What is something that you always say yes to that you really want to say "no" to?

_____

_____

A client whose abuser had performed oral sex on her was struggling to engage in this act with her boyfriend. We spent quite some time doing the work to separate the experience she had with the abuser from her current, present-day relationship. When she was ready, she agreed to spend as much time as she needed looking at her boyfriend to ground herself in the present and saying her declaration—"It is my choice"—before asking him to go down on her. She decided to make a clear request as to which areas were "off limits" and that she only wanted it to last five minutes. A few months later, she happily reported, "I can't believe it! I chose to ask him go down on me for a half hour, and I felt so present and relaxed."

Your sex life will not change overnight. I get that these are tough issues—after all, being naked and engaged with another person is just about as vulnerable and intimate as it gets. You can, though, begin reclaiming sex as fun, exciting, satisfying, ridiculous, breathtaking, playful, erotic, kinky, fulfilling *(add your own adjectives:* _____ *)* by owning the fact that you get to choose when, with whom, and how.

By the way, if you are single, you actually get to choose the type of sex you have *with yourself* as well!

It is about choice not obligation.

Homework

Pay close attention to your attitude and behaviors toward sex. Practice choosing and specifically say "yes" to one thing and say "no" to one thing and journal about the experience. How might your attitudes toward and responses to sex transform if you embraced your right to choose and let go of obligation?

PART 9
MOVING ON

Lesson 30
Forgiveness

As we near the end of our journey, we turn our attention to a very important step in recovery: forgiveness.

One major obstacle that stands in the way of our forgiving the abuser is that we have all the wrong ideas about what it means to forgive in the first place. It is important to understand that forgiveness (from *Shelter from the Storm*):

- Does not mean the abuse was okay
- Does not mean the person has permission to hurt you again
- Does not mean the offense was not great
- Does not depend on the abuser saying she or he is sorry
- Does not mean that the offense was not deliberate or repeated

We often fall into the false belief that forgiveness means letting the abuser off the hook and accepting the injustice of it all. Quite the contrary, forgiveness is about letting *ourselves* off the hook! Both the Greek and the Hebrew verbs for forgive can also be translated "to send away." **Forgiveness is about sending away the hurt, pain, anger, and bitterness and taking back our life.** We also send away the abuser and his or her hold upon our thoughts, emotions, and experiences in the present day.

Most importantly, forgiveness is a choice, not a feeling. Since it is a choice, making a decision to forgive can be arrived at by examining both our reasons for and against forgiving the abuser (this is similar to looking for the payoffs and costs).

Spend some time reflecting on your reasons for and against forgiving, but, first, consider what Kubetin-Littlefield has to say on the matter:

> *"... many of us mistakenly believe that unforgiveness will somehow hurt those who hurt us. By refusing to offer forgiveness, we hope to 'get even' with them. But the opposite is true. Abusers, unforgiven, go right on doing what they do. They never considered us in the first place, and our unforgiveness has absolutely no [effect] on their behavior."*

> —Cynthia Kubetin-Littlefield, *Shelter from the Storm*

My reasons not to forgive:

_____

_____

My reasons to forgive:

_____

_____

_____

_____

There are some very real consequences of choosing not to forgive. Watch the clips from **Woman Thou Art Loosed** (Tracks 7 & 8) and then answer the following questions. In Scene 1, we meet Michelle, who is twelve years old. Her mother's boyfriend has just arrived home and attacks Michelle (*contains sensitive material that may be triggering*).

In Scene 2, Michelle has grown up, but had a very hard life, including jail time. This scene begins with a visit from her parole officer.

From Scene 1, what did you feel as you watched Michelle? What did you notice about her?

_____

_____

What did you notice about the abuser?

_____

_____

How did you feel about the mother's reaction in the moment Michelle told her what happened?

_____

_____

What stories do you think Michelle walked away with given her mother's response?

_____

_____

As the mother explained her story, did it change the way you viewed her response to Michelle?

_____

_____

From Scene 2, can you relate to Michelle's feeling of being "owed" something?

_____

_____

What are the consequences of not forgiving for Michelle?

_____

_____

What are the consequences for you of not forgiving?

_____

_____

One of the main lessons we learn from Michelle's story is that we have the opportunity to look ahead and not behind, to leave our pain and hurt "at the altar" so to speak. In order to do this, we first need to understand that (from *Shelter from the Storm*):

- You cannot genuinely forgive until you acknowledge the full scope and impact of the offense.
- You cannot forgive and deny the offense at the same time.
- You cannot forgive someone else for an offense and carry responsibility for that same offense yourself.
- You cannot carry shame for an offense yourself and at the same time forgive someone else for it.

Use the worksheet, **Leaving It All Behind** (Appendix J), to write down all of the things you are ready to leave behind and to forgive. If you struggle with the word "forgive," reframe the issue and think of it as deciding what you want to release or let go of from the past.

Finally, share some words or feelings that come to mind when you think of your abuser ...

_____

_____

Now, turn back to Lesson 12 where you did this exercise before. Take some time to reflect upon what is different now and what has stayed the same.

What do you notice?

_____

_____

_____

Forgiving the abuser needs to precede entering into a conversation with him or her about what happened. In the next lesson, we will discuss how to have a conversation with the abuser if that is something you feel strongly about doing.

Homework

Find a moment to read over your "Leaving It All Behind" worksheet. After reflecting and truly committing to leaving it behind, dispose of the list in some way that feels meaningful to you, e.g., burn it, shred it, toss it into the ocean.

Lesson 31
Conversation with the Abuser

In the world of recovery, there is a lot written on the topic of *confronting* the abuser. However, as I thought about this step of recovery (by the way, it is not one that is required in order to live Beyond Surviving), I was struck by how counterproductive it is to use the word "confrontation." By definition, confrontation is about meeting someone face-to-face with a *hostile or argumentative intent*. That just feels all wrong to me, especially since:

1. One of the ways to have this conversation is through simulation rather than face-to-face.

2. At this point in recovery, I hope that expressing hostility toward the abuser is not at the top of your list.

3. What is there to argue about or debate? Our purpose is not to offer the abuser an opportunity to argue his or her case nor is it our purpose to argue our position.

In addition, think back to all that we have learned so far about framing our experiences by considering what we are out to prove, who we are being, and who we have others being. If we sit down with the abuser with a hostile and argumentative attitude, then the starting point of confrontation clearly directs the experience toward anger, distrust, animosity, etc. We end up experiencing the interaction as a battle, one that we have to win in order to feel validated.

When we enter into a conversation rather than a confrontation, our focus will be on communicating our thoughts and feelings rather than winning an argument. Therefore, the conversation is not about persuading or convincing the abuser to say or do anything, it is about sharing our story with the person(s) involved in order to break the silence and release the hold of the past on our life.

A conversation is all about the exchange of information, thoughts, and ideas—now this is at the heart of the matter. A conversation provides us an opportunity to:

- Release the emotions about the abuse and regain the power lost to the abuser
- Deal with the person who abused us in a way that honors our power and recovery
- Open the door to a new relationship and reconciliation with the abuser
- Express our feelings about the effects of the abuse and about the abuser

Alternatively, the conversation cannot be used to:

- Vindicate or validate our experiences, thoughts, feelings
- Regain the relationship that was lost in the past
- Provide a reason to forgive based on how the abuser responds
- Manipulate the abuser into apologizing or acknowledging what happened
- Embarrass or shame the abuser
- Force the abuser to take responsibility for the abuse

Reflection

Aside from the reasons already listed, what reasons do you have for having a conversation with the abuser?

_____

_____

_____

_____

What feelings arise when you consider having this conversation?

_____

_____

What thoughts arise when you think about having this conversation?

_____

_____

Now let's explore the two types of conversations that we can have—it is actually pretty straightforward. The in-person conversation consists of a face-to-face experience, whereas a simulated conversation consists of talking to an empty chair or picture of the abuser or writing a letter.

Determining which type of conversation to have depends on a few factors:

- Is the abuser still alive or someone whom you have access to?
- Is it safe to have a face-to-face conversation with the abuser? Is there a chance the abuser would become extraordinarily agitated or violent?
- Are your motivations for having an in-person conversation healthy?
- Do you have the proper support system in place if the in-person conversation results in violence, retaliation, loss of the relationship, or other negative outcomes? Is there someone who could go with you?
- Do you have the proper support system in place to process the emotions that arise during and after a simulated or in-person conversation?

It is important to reiterate here that we do not need to have either of these conversations—in-person or simulated—in order to recover and heal from the abuse. There is value in stating out loud to the abuser (in-person or simulated) the impact of their actions on our life, but all of the work we have done already is the meat of the journey. A conversation with the abuser can add to our recovery, but it can also cause more harm than good if we are not prepared for how the abuser might respond or we do not have a clear game plan.

There are typically three ways that abusers respond. First, there is remorse. The abuser feels guilty or ashamed, is aware of the damage the abuse caused, and is relieved to have an opportunity to discuss what happened and ask for forgiveness.

Secondly, there is denial. The abuser refuses outright to acknowledge that anything happened, claims we are making things up or remembering incorrectly, and will often turn things back on us by accusing us of trying to harm them in some way.

Finally, there is rationalization. The abuser acknowledges that abuse occurred, but excuses it by either claiming it was not wrong, it was for our own good, or that it was not that big of a deal.

When preparing for an in-person conversation, it is important to first:

- Be really sure that you are not rushing this step of recovery—the conversation needs to take place when the time is right, when you feel grounded and strong in who you are and the truth of your experience.
- Be "prepared to state the offense clearly and calmly, to stand firm in the fact that the behavior was abusive, and to refuse to take responsibility for it" (*Shelter from the Storm*). Remember, you are not there to defend your position or convince the abuser of anything.
- Have a strong support system in place during and after the conversation.
- Be ready to deal with any of the three typical responses: remorse, denial, rationalization.
- Spend some time preparing for the conversation and have a game plan (we will explore that a bit more below).

If you decide to have a simulated conversation, it is important to have the first three items from above in place as well.

If you decide to have an in-person conversation, you need to develop a game plan.

Step 1: Get clear about why you want to have the conversation.

What are your goals? (Remember, only list things you can control.)

_____

_____

_____

_____

Step 2: Create a support system.

Who will go with you? Who will you call before and after the conversation? What clear requests can you make of the person(s) so they can best support you?

_____

_____

Step 3: Acknowledge what you most hope will happen as a result of the conversation.

What do you hope the abuser will say or do? (Remember, these are things you cannot control.)

_____

_____

_____

_____

Step 4: Put aside what you hope the abuser will say or do and get clear about your role in the conversation.

Who do you want to be in the conversation? When the conversation is over, what do you want to be able to say about yourself?

_____

_____

_____

_____

Step 5: Be prepared for worst-case scenarios.

What could the abuser say or do that could really hurt you or others? How will you handle it if that happens? How will you handle it if your abuser responds with remorse, denial, or rationalization?

_____

_____

_____

_____

Step 6: Explore alternative ways to satisfy your desires and needs if the abuser either expresses denial or rationalization.

How could you meet your needs and desires independent of the abuser?

Example: Have a close friend say the things you had hoped the abuser would say, write a letter in the voice of the abuser saying all the things you wanted to hear, etc.

_____

_____

It is important not to skip over any of these steps before you have the conversation with the abuser. Role-playing and practicing the conversation are great ways to set yourself up for success!

Take some time now to watch the clip from **Searching for Angela Shelton** (Track 9) *(contains sensitive material that may be triggering)*. In this scene, Angela is "confronting" her father who abused her. (I also highly encourage you to purchase the full-length movie as well—it is an amazing film!)

What did you notice about Angela as she prepared for talking with her father?

_____

_____

What did you notice about Angela during the confrontation?

_____

_____

What thoughts or feelings did you have as you watched Angela's father respond? How would you characterize his response (e.g., remorse, denial, or rationalization)?

_____

_____

Which steps of the game plan do you think Angela did or did not do to prepare?

_____

_____

Now watch this second clip from **Searching for Angela Shelton** (Track 10) *(contains sensitive material that may be triggering)*. In this scene, Angela is having a "conversation" with her step-brother who also abused her and her sister.

What do you notice about this interaction? How is it different from the interaction she has with her father?

_____

_____

_____

Regardless of whether we decide to have a conversation with the abuser or not, we are free to live a life that we love, to live powerfully, to release the hold that the abuse has had on our thoughts and behavior, and to step into living Beyond Surviving from this day forward!

Homework

If you are ready for an in-person or simulated conversation, spend some time fully developing your game plan. If you are not, do not make yourself bad or wrong—just tuck this away should the day come when you need it.

PART 10
WRAPPING IT ALL UP

Lesson 32
Celebration!

Every journey comes to an end, and I hope that you are finding yourself at the end of this journey filled with power, optimism, hope, and healing.

It has been an honor to go on this journey with you. I acknowledge you for the courage, commitment, and integrity that you have exhibited. You have taken on your past, you have faced your false beliefs and patterns of behavior, and you have broken the silence.

Before we say good-bye, let's spend a little time considering where you have been and where you are going!

Spend ten minutes reflecting on who you were on day one. What were your stories? How did you feel mentally, emotionally, and physically?

_____

_____

_____

_____

_____

_____

Now, spend ten minutes reflecting on who you are today. At this point in time, what do you know and believe about yourself?

_____

_____

_____

_____

_____

_____

What measurable results have you achieved?

_____

_____

_____

_____

Which measurable results do you still need to do some work on?

_____

_____

_____

_____

How will you use what you have learned in the future?

_____

_____

_____

_____

List three things that you would like to continue working on and how you will go about doing so:

_____

_____

_____

I encourage you to review the **Key Concepts** (Appendix K) that we have covered and even keep them nearby to refer to from time to time. Also check out the **References** and **Suggestions for Further Reading** sections at the end of the guidebook.

Most importantly, celebrate and acknowledge the journey you have taken and all that you have gained as a result. It is no small thing what you have accomplished!

When you have a hard day, and there will be hard days when your stories seem to overwhelm you, do not distress! Just return to the skills and tools you have learned to regain your balance and grounding.

I hope you will fully step into all that is possible and available to you now. You no longer have to be trapped by the patterns of thought and behavior that came about because of the abuse.

There was a time when choices were made for you, but being a Beyond Survivor is about taking back your right and responsibility to choose. You have the opportunity now to powerfully choose how you will respond to situations, what you will prove, how you will deal with the abuser, who you will connect with and how, and to communicate your needs and desires. From this moment forward, you truly are the author of your life!

And, always remember, what you think, you create!

APPENDICES

Appendix A:
Commitment for Individuals

I understand that:

1. Sessions will start at the scheduled time and end on time. My regular attendance and prompt arrival is expected, and I commit myself to the entire session. I will let my coach know if I will be late as soon as it is obvious that this will be the case.

2. If I am unable to attend a session, I will contact my coach 24 hours in advance.

3. If I should choose to drop out of the program, I will come back for one more session and share with my coach why I am leaving.

4. The purpose of the program is not solely to gain knowledge, but to also apply and experience transformation in my life.

5. I will do the session activities, any homework, and participate in the coaching sessions, because I need the comfort, motivation, insight, and support in tackling complex issues as I seek help in my recovery process.

6. I will in no way hold my coach or anyone else legally responsible for any actions I might take against myself or others.

7. I will complete a One Month Follow-Up evaluation form.

8. I will complete a One Year Follow-Up evaluation form.

I agree to commit myself to these principles.

Signature: _____ Date: _____

Appendix B:
Guidelines for Individuals

Respect Yourself

Self-Focus: You are here to learn about and work on yourself.

Listen: It is everyone's responsibility to "tune in."

Take Responsibility: You have a voice in this journey. You are completely free to bring up issues and concerns about the program or me.

Respect Others

Stay on the Subject: During sessions, we will focus on issues having to do with sexual abuse and the outcomes and effects of the abuse. For the sake of time, I may interrupt if we seem to be getting off track.

Minimize Distractions: Please take care to minimize noise, interruptions, or multitasking during sessions. Focus on being fully engaged and present.

I agree to commit myself to these guidelines for each session.

Signature: _____ Date: _____

Appendix C:
Commitment for Course

I understand that:

1. The sessions will start and end on time. My regular attendance and prompt arrival is expected, and I commit myself to the entire session. I will let my coach know if I will be late.

2. I will have a 15-minute phone call with my coach each week.

3. I understand that missing sessions will greatly impact the effectiveness of the course. If I have to miss a session, I will contact my coach before the session.

4. I understand that I may not miss more than two sessions. If I am unable to fulfill my commitment to the course regarding attendance, I will be asked to stop attending and will have an opportunity to participate in a future course.

5. If I should choose to drop out of the course, I will come back for one more session and share why I am leaving. This will bring closure and help the other participants deal with any feelings of rejection or abandonment.

6. The purpose of the course is not solely to gain knowledge, but to also apply and experience transformation in my life.

7. I will do the session activities, any homework, and participate in the discussions, because I need the comfort, motivation, insight, and support in tackling complex issues as I seek help in my recovery process.

8. I will in no way hold the coach or anyone else in the course legally responsible for any actions I might take against myself or others. I understand this course is not meant to replace therapeutic diagnosis or interventions that may be appropriate for me.

9. I will complete a One Month Follow-Up evaluation form.

10. I will complete a One Year Follow-Up evaluation form.

I agree to commit myself to these principles.

Signature: _____ Date: _____

Appendix D: Guidelines for Course

Respect Yourself

Self-Focus: We are here to learn about and work on ourselves. We will share our own experiences, insights, and feelings.

Listen: It is everyone's responsibility to "tune in." This includes listening to someone's words, being sensitive to the feelings they express, and paying attention to your reactions as the other person communicates.

Take Responsibility: We all have a voice in this course. You are completely free to bring up issues and concerns about the course, other participants, or me.

Respect Others

Be on Time: It is important that you not distract others by showing up late or unprepared. This includes coming back from breaks at the designated time.

Stay on the Subject: During course time, we will focus on issues having to do with sexual abuse and the outcomes and effects of the abuse. We will definitely have time before or after sessions to socialize.

Minimize Distractions: Please always turn off cell phones and use the restroom before each session. There will be scheduled breaks, but if you do need to go to the restroom during a session, please let me know.

Communication: Each person knows she or he will have a chance to be heard, because we will all make an effort not to monopolize the conversation.

I agree to commit myself to these guidelines for each session.

Signature: _____ Date: _____

Appendix E: Confidentiality for Course

Confidentiality is a must in a Beyond Surviving Course! My goal is to provide you with a safe and supportive environment in which to share and heal.

Confidentiality is based on cooperation of all course participants to maintain it. However, the course leader has no power to enforce what a course participant chooses to do outside of the course. If a participant chooses to break the confidence of any participant sharing in the course, she or he may jeopardize her or his participation in the course. The ability to keep a confidence is one of the requirements for course participation. We adopt together the following general rule and expectation to protect and maintain course trust and confidentiality:

I agree to maintain the confidence of each person in this Beyond Surviving Course. I will not disclose outside the course anything that is shared within it. Exceptions would be: 1) If your leader has reasonable cause to believe that a course participant is a danger to him/herself or others; and 2) During course supervision, your course leader may share some of the course processes in order to receive instruction, guidance, and direction for your benefit and that of the course. Participants' names will not be used if at all possible.

I have read and understand the principles and limits of confidentiality for this Beyond Surviving Course. I will respect and keep the confidences of all the course participants.

Signature: _____ Date: _____

Appendix F:
My Plan for Managing Crisis

I must learn to ask for help and be willing to accept help when it is offered. When I feel overwhelmed with my emotions, anxiety, depression, or suicidal thoughts, I will contact the following individual(s):

I will call _____ at _____.

If that person is not available,

I will call _____ at _____.

When I am feeling overwhelmed or that I can't handle things, I will center and ground myself by ...

_____

_____

_____

_____

Appendix G:
Completion Log

Item to Complete	Do By	Done?

Appendix H:
Positive Data Log

What I have been proving: _____

What I am out to prove instead: _____

Pay attention to the evidence that supports what you are out to prove instead and log it here:

Date	Evidence that supports what I am out to prove

Appendix I:
Payoffs & Costs

Behavior, Attitude, Way of Being	Payoff	Cost

Appendix J:
Leaving It All Behind

Today, I am leaving behind, letting go of ...

_____

_____

_____

_____

_____

_____

_____

_____

_____

Today, I am forgiving myself for, releasing ...

_____

_____

_____

_____

Today, I am forgiving my abuser for ...

_____

_____

_____

_____

Appendix K:
Key Concepts

What Happened vs. Story

Continue practicing separating the facts of a situation from your interpretation.

Meaning Making

Somebody said _____, and I made it mean _____.

Making Clear Requests

Be specific. You are giving a gift to the people in your life when you give them clear information about what you need. This also allows you to more easily evaluate the relationship.

Measurable Results

Identify the symptom. What is occurring, what is your current experience? Create a measurable result (time limited and specific). How will you track, measure your progress? How will you reward yourself?

You Have to Be It—Not Do It

We cannot transform by trying to "do" something different. First address your mind (thoughts), which changes your word (speak/declaration), which then changes your experience (do).

What Do You Want to Prove?

Anything can be proven true. Decide want you want to prove about yourself, others, and relationships.

Payoffs & Costs for Every Way of Being

Every behavior has costs and payoffs. The reason a behavior remains is because of the perceived payoffs. By getting present to what the behavior is costing us, we can take a step toward transforming our ways of being.

Who Do You Have People Being?

We often determine who others will be (the perfect man) or what others will do (people always leave). We limit our view of others and stifle possibility when we say "He/she is ____." Remember to always check for whether you are limiting possibilities.

Stop Pretending

I pretend to be _____ to cover up that I am _____.

Feelings Are Just Feelings!

Feelings should not dictate our lives. Instead, what we have given our word to—integrity—should guide us. Feelings should not be completely ignored (there is a time to trust your instincts). There is a difference, however, between trusting your instincts and getting stuck or stopped because of how you feel.

Trust Trap

No one is 100 percent trustworthy. Our job is to decide whether or not to trust someone by considering their behavior and speech as signals of their beliefs, values, and intentions, which are all indications of what commitments they are willing to keep, how often, and for how long.

Intimacy

Private and personal detailed knowledge obtained by much study or experience. There is always risk.

Sex Is a Choice, Not an Obligation!

Forgiveness Is a Choice

Also, remember, until you assign the blame or responsibility to the abuser, you have nothing to forgive!

Appendix L: Media Guide

Track	Title
1	Jessica's Daily Affirmation
2	Scene from Good Will Hunting
3	Poem by Staceyann Chin
4	It's All About Perception
5	Be Who You Were Meant to Be
6	The Power of Vulnerability
7	Woman Thou Art Loosed—Scene 1
8	Woman Thou Art Loosed—Scene 2
9	Searching for Angela Shelton—Scene 1
10	Searching for Angela Shelton—Scene 2

Go to www.rachelgrantcoaching.com/videos to view the above tracks

References

Books

Blume, E. Sue. *Secret Survivors*. New York: Ballantine Books, 1991.

Chichester Clark, Emma. *Amazing Mr. Zooty!*. London: Andersen Press, 2007.

Frankl, Viktor. *Man's Search for Meaning*. Boston: Beacon Press, 2006.

Kubetin-Littlefield, and James Mallory. *Shelter from the Storm: Hope for Survivors of Sexual Abuse*. Nashville: Lifeway Christian Resources, 1995.

Jones, Dan. "How to Be Happy." *New Scientist,* September 22, 2010.

Lewis, C.S. *Mere Christianity*. New York: Macmillan, 1960.

Rubin, Gretchen. *The Happiness Project*. New York: HarperCollins, 2011.

Siegel, Daniel. *The Developing Mind: How Relationships and the Brain Interact to Shape Who We Are*. New York: The Guilford Press, 2012.

Smith, Huston. *The Religions of Man*. New York: HarperCollins, 1965.

Movies

Good Will Hunting. Directed by Gus Van Sant. Santa Monica, CA: Miramax Films, 1997. DVD.

Searching for Angela Shelton. Directed by Angela Shelton. Beverly Hills, CA: Liberty International, 2004. DVD.

Woman Thou Art Loosed. Directed by Michael Schultz. Los Angeles, CA: 20th Century Fox, 2005. DVD.

Suggestions for Further Reading

Books—Nonfiction

Bennett, Bija. *Emotional Yoga: How the Body Can Heal the Mind*. New York: Fireside, 2002.

Berman, Jennifer and Laura Berman. *For Women Only: A Revolutionary Guide to Overcoming Sexual Dysfunction and Reclaiming Your Sex Life*. New York: Henry Holt & Company, 2001.

Carter, Les, and Frank Minirth. *The Anger Workbook*. Nashville: Thomas Nelson, 1992.

Chapman, Constance. *Am I Worth It? How to Turn Doubt Into YES Forever*. Seattle: Createspace, 2011.

Clubb, John Mark. *Boys Cry Too: A Story of Hope, Forgiveness, Redemption and Change*. Seattle: Createspace, 2009.

Crabb, Larry. *The Marriage Builder*. New York: Zondervan, 1992.

Davidson, Jeff. *60 Second Self-Starter*. Avon: Adams Media, 2008.

De Becker, Gavin. *The Gift of Fear*. New York: Donadio & Ashworth, 1998.

Emerson, David and Elizabeth Hopper. *Overcoming Trauma through Yoga*. Berkeley: North Atlantic Books, 2012.

Gottman, John. *The Seven Principles for Making Marriage Work*. New York: Three Rivers Press, 1999.

Kane, Richard. *Bronx Street Kid*. Bloomington: AuthorHouse, 2012.

Krainin, Cynthia, and Nancy Brook. *Thriving at Work: A Guidebook for Survivors of Sexual Abuse*. Lowell: King Publishing, 2006.

Haines, Staci. *The Survivor's Guide to Sex: How to Have an Empowered Sex Life After Childhood Sexual Abuse*. Berkeley: Cleis Press, 1999.

McKinnon, Marjorie. *Repair Your Life*. Ann Arbor: Loving Healing Press, 2011.

Meyers, Joyce. *Battlefield of the Mind: Winning the Battle in Your Mind*. Nashville: Faithwords, 2002.

Meyers, Joyce. *Beauty for Ashes*. Tulsa: Harrison House Inc., 1994.

O'Donnell, Rebecca. *Freak: The True Story of an Insecurity Addict*. Bloomington: iUniverse, 2011.

Parrot, Andrea. *Coping with Date Rape and Acquaintance Rape*. New York: Rosen Publishing Group, 1993.

Pillow, Larry. *Family and Friends: Helping the Person You Care About in Recovery*. Nashville: Lifeway Publishing, 1995.

Shelton, Angela. *Be Your Own Hero Warrior Workbook*. Seattle: Createspace, 2011.

Strong, Mary. *Letters of the Scattered Brotherhood*. New York: HarperOne, 1991.

Wray Gregoire, Sheila. *Honey, I Don't Have a Headache Tonight*. Grand Rapids: Kregel Publications, 2004.

Zilbergeld, Bernie. *The New Male Sexuality: The Truth About Men, Sex, and Pleasure*. New York: Bantam, 1999.

Books—Fiction

Fontaine, Claire. *Come Back: A Mother and Daughter's Journey Through Hell and Back*. New York: Harper Perennial, 2007.

Lamb, Wally. *She's Come Undone*. New York: Washington Square Press, 1996.

Millman, Dan. *Way of the Peaceful Warrior*. Tiburon: H.J. Kramer, Inc., 1984.

Online Resources

Pandora's Aquarium: If you have been a victim of any type of sexual violence, you belong here. Join their community and take full advantage of what this online support group has to offer you as you heal and recover.

http://pandys.org/forums/

SexLiesandConsciousness: a blogtalkradio show hosted by Executive Coach, Mai Vu, The Voice of Healthy Sex. The shows are daring, meaningful and aim to reclaim OUR sex, so that we can regain our freedom, our choices around our sex.

http://www.blogtalkradio.com/sexliesandconsciousness

Surviving Spirit: a non-profit organization dedicated to promoting hope, healing, and help for those impacted by trauma, abuse, or mental health concerns through the use of the creative arts, a speakers' bureau, newsletter, website, brochure, retail gallery, coffeehouse, media center, and more.

http://www.survivingspirit.com

About the Author

Rachel Grant is a trauma recovery coach and earned a master's degree in counseling psychology. With training in human behavior and cognitive development, she provides a compassionate and challenging approach for her clients while using coaching as opposed to therapeutic models. When not working with clients, she is dancing, reading, or at the theater. She lives in San Francisco, California.